Experimental Textiles

Experimental Textiles

A journey through design, interpretation and inspiration

Kim Thittichai

BATSFORD

Dedication

This book is dedicated to Chris Field, without whose help and encouragement the course Experimental Textiles would never have run. Chris was instrumental in the training and development of hundreds of adult education tutors and helped me to write the third and fourth levels of my course. She was a very good friend and is greatly missed.

Acknowledgments

I would like to thank all of my students, who have been my inspiration for this book; we have all worked hard and had great fun together.

I would also like to thank all the professional tutors and artists who have allowed their work to be used in this book.

First published in the United Kingdom in 2009 by
Batsford
10 Southcombe Street
London W14 0RA

An imprint of Anova Books Company Ltd

ISBN 9781906388478

A CIP catalogue record for this book is available from the British Library.

16 15 14 13 12 10 09 08
10 9 8 7 6 5 4 3 2 1

Repro by Rival Colour Ltd, UK
Printed by Craft Print International Ltd, Singapore

This book can be ordered direct from the publisher at the website: www.anovabooks.com, or try your local bookshop.

Distributed in the United States and Canada by
Sterling Publishing Co.,
387 Park Avenue South, New York, NY 10016, USA

Opposite: 'Gormanghast' casket by Carol Coleman, made from impressed softsculpt, thermoplastic foam and decorated with fabrics, beads and embroidery. To see the inside of the casket, turn to page 83.

Contents

Introduction

'Experience is what you get when you don't get what you want.'
Dan Stanford

Like many people my age I have had several career changes in my life but what, I hope, is my final one has given me the most satisfaction. I have been teaching in adult education since 1996, not as long as many tutors perhaps, but I have learned a lot along the way. The most important thing I have learned is that anyone can be taught or teach themselves techniques; it is what you do with them that makes your work different.

Having spent a lot of time teaching and lecturing to various groups, one of the things that stands out for me, particularly over the past two years, is that a lot of us are being seduced by the latest technique, tools or equipment and forgetting the basics of design, colour and composition. Books of samples are all very well – but then what?

Getting back to basics once in a while is very important, to refresh old skills and remind yourself of the value of observation, applying colour and just taking time to think about what you are doing rather than rushing into the latest craze. If you work on your own it can be difficult to find the time and the inclination to generate new ideas. If you have not had the benefit of undertaking a suitable college course you may not know how to begin. Even if you have, taking time out to reinforce old learning can feel like time wasted, but this is far from the truth.

This book is named after a 30-week course I wrote and taught for seven years in the south of England. 'Experimental Textiles' was originally written as a one-year course but my students just would not leave and so eventually it developed into a four-year course being taught in two separate colleges. The course was so popular that it became necessary to run several first and second years to cope with the demand. The idea was to teach all the basic skills required to develop and encourage the students to work independently as textile artists.

Right: Heavily beaded and machine-stitched 'Sea Horse' by Nikki Parmenter.

When you write a course and it is advertized in the college prospectus, there is no guarantee that it will run. All colleges have a minimum number of students that must be enrolled before the course can run and the magic number at our college was 12. The first year only one student enrolled; the second year eight enrolled. By this time I doubted that the course would ever run and that something I believed in so strongly was not necessarily what others needed. Chris Field, Curriculum Leader at the Connaught Centre (an adult education centre in Hove, Sussex), who later helped me write the higher levels of the course, encouraged me to advertize my course for the third time. The course enrolled enough students and it ran. It just goes to show that if you believe enough in what you are doing and hang on in there, there is a chance your wishes will come true.

The course was broken into three ten-week terms: the first two terms covered design, colour and textile techniques; the last term was set aside for the students to design, create and finish a piece of work to be hung at the end-of-year show.

The first year covered basic design and colour theory, along with all the basic textile techniques from rag rugging and felt-making to working with metal. The second year developed the skills learned in the first year. In the third and fourth years students began to consider their professional development with personal projects becoming more important. As with all good things, the course had to come to an end, as it was not possible to keep up with the number of students who wanted to attend. Before I started winding down Experimental Textiles I was teaching ten groups across four levels. I had taken on too much. It was a classic case of 'be careful what you wish for'.

This book will take you from design, through interpretation and inspiration to encourage you to stop thinking about it and get on with it.

While reading the following pages you will find many references to working in groups, particularly for the exercises. This is an excellent way to broaden the range of your experience and ideas but in no way negates the value of working on your own. If you are experimenting with textiles on your own but would like input or to share your ideas with others, take a look on the internet. There are many blogs put up by like-minded souls who are creating marvellous work.

Inspiration is a very personal issue. It is not possible to have one rule or formula for everyone. I hope that the projects and information in this book may give you some new ideas and help inspire you.

The artists that I have chosen to include have all inspired me in one way or another. I have been a student of some, and a teacher or a colleague of others and I have admired them all. I hope they all give you something to think about. Contact details for the artists are at the back of the book.

Right: Felted bag by Mary Dean. Made with hand-rolled felt incorporating vintage fabrics and threads and finished with hand-rolled pom pons. The bag is 61x 38cm (24 x 15in).

Please bear in mind that this book is just my interpretation of what I have learned on my relatively short journey as a tutor. It is intended as a starting point for you to begin your research into what interests you most. There are many excellent tutors who have longer experience; seek them out and work with them and above all listen to them! Don't just stick to textiles; you can be taught to draw and paint, it's just a matter of confidence.

Part One

Where Do Ideas Come From?

Recording ideas

We are always being told to keep a sketchbook. If you are attending a course at college you will be encouraged to use sketchbooks, folders and portfolios to store your work. However, what is right for one person isn't necessarily right for the next. If you are experimenting with three-dimensional samples, for example, several shoeboxes or cardboard boxes might be more useful than a sketchbook that bulges and then falls apart. The main thing is that you keep a record of your work and have some means of storing it safely.

There are many different types of books that are useful for storing information; softback, hardback, spiral-bound, white pages, black pages, fat and thin. What is important is that you choose what is right for you, not something that everyone else is using or that you think looks good. Stop and think for a moment. What are you using a sketchbook for? Would you rather use a scrapbook? A sketchbook always sounds so important, so if you are at all worried about committing ideas to paper perhaps you might prefer to get a basic scrapbook and fill it with ideas. These are widely available and are usually softback with cheap coloured sugar-paper pages. They are excellent for sticking in photos and images cut from magazines, scribbled notes and sketches, old handouts, interesting (dried) plant life you have picked up on a walk – anything that sparks an idea. A scrapbook is often seen as less threatening than a sketchbook.

Left: Hardback sketchbook painted with Procion dye powder and water. If you thought the plain white sketchbook was daunting, this may inspire you.

There are many forms of commercial sketchbooks. They come in many shapes, sizes and layouts, often with a choice of paper, but as a rule the pages are white.

There are few things as daunting as blank sheet of white paper, particularly when it is contained in a sketchbook. What are you supposed to put in a sketchbook? Does it have to be a beautifully finished work of art or can it just be a useful record of ideas, lists and scratchy drawings? How you use a sketchbook is totally up to you. Don't be intimidated by others who create a masterpiece of exquisite pages that are highly embellished and decorated. A sketchbook should not be an end in itself but more a doorway or first step towards an idea or range of work.

One of the most popular ways of changing the pages I have found is to paint an entire sketchbook in one go with a dilute solution of Procion dye powder and water. Procion dyes are used to dye natural fabrics and although when dying fabrics, in order to make the dye fast and washable, you add a fix, this is not necessary with paper as you are not going to wash it. Just mix a little dye powder with water and paint onto the pages (when mixing dye powders you should wear a particle mask). Use lots of different colours and a wide paintbrush and see how they bleed together. Paint a page at a time until the whole book is done, and then close the book. You will have a lovely wet mess that will take ages to dry but it will be worth it. Once the book is dry or just damp, carefully separate the pages. You will find that they do not stick together. This would not be the case if you were to use ink or paint to colour the pages.

Now you have a wonderful array of coloured pages on which to write notes, stick photos, draw onto and generally let rip.

Below: A concertina sketchbook before it was painted and after.

Getting started

Why not set yourself a project and collect images of all the spirals you can find? You could do this as a group project and create an exhibition of work that was inspired by the research. There are two different types of spiral – the Archimedes spiral, which is the shape a spider creates when spinning its web, or the way a sailor coils his rope, which is the equiangular spiral and the way that some plants or shells grow. Have a look at a Brussels sprout, a pine cone and an artichoke and see if you can discern which spiral describes the way each one grows.

This project could be developed to include fractals, honeycombs or patterns of flow as in rivers and ripples or lines left in the sand by the tide. Once you start to look it is quite amazing where you can find certain shapes.

A popular sketchbook project could be 'Marks Made by Man'. This could be interpreted in many ways: footprints in the sand, motorways through a landscape, tribal scarring and tattoos, the list is endless. Again, have a look about you; you may surprise yourself.

Why are you storing information?

It is so important to store your ideas and experiments. It is even better if you can write them up. Yes, I know it is boring, and you are always in a hurry to get on with the next new and exciting technique or project. Stop for a minute, grab a pen and just make some quick notes, to record what you are doing. Even if it hasn't worked out how you imagined, the information may be useful later on.

A distinction needs to be made between a working sketch/scrapbook and something more finished and beautiful. There is a danger when working in these books of trying so hard to make your book look lovely that you 'wear out' your original idea. You need a certain amount of creative energy to devise, create and finish a project. If you spend a lot of time and energy on your sketch/scrapbook there may well be little or nothing left for your project. A working sketch/scrapbook should be a tool, not a finished masterpiece. Do not confuse making a finished book with a work in progress.

Having a folder or scrapbook of work to look back on even in two or three years time can help when you are feeling less than inspired.

It could be a colour combination you need or a particular layered technique that you created and thought you would never need again. You just never know. We have all discovered by now that we never know what is round the corner, so bear this in mind when you are having a good clear out.

Below: A selection of sketchbooks. The type of sketchbook you choose is a matter of need and personal preference. Alternatively, keep your work in a box or folder.

My piece entitled 'Capstones' (below) was inspired by a photograph I had taken in Camelford, Cornwall. I was mindlessly flipping through an old sketchbook and came across the original sketches I had made, along with the photograph. It was just what I had been looking for as a wall-hung piece for an exhibition. The result was 'Capstones', 213 × 91cm (7 × 3ft). Sections of Pelmet Vilene were painted with acrylic paint and then stitched onto a black cotton background. This was then stretched over a wooden frame to create a sharp line. I did not want anything to detract from the image, so I used a very simple process. You do not need to get complicated and throw lots of techniques at a piece of work if you are going for simplicity and impact. It can actually take longer to produce something simple as it has to be right and you can spend hours just moving a part of your work little bit this way and a little bit that way until you get it right. This, of course, means that it is right in your eyes; someone else could come along and suggest something different again. It is all a matter of opinion.

Opposite: A photograph of a wall in Cornwall. I used this photograph, along with my original sketches, as references for 'Capstones' (below).

Below: 'Capstones' by Kim Thittichai. Pelmet Vilene was painted with acrylic paint and Procion dye and stitched to a black cotton background. The piece measures 213 x 91cm (7 x 3ft)

Creating Original Designs

What makes one person's work different from the next? How can you create work that will stand out from the crowd? While it is generally true that if you give a group of people the same project and similar materials they will all create something different, we all strive to find that original formula that works for us.

Having taught both accredited and non-accredited courses I have learnt the importance of using primary sources.

Primary sources tend to be original drawings, sketches or artworks. This means something you have generated and developed.

Secondary sources are photographs, postcards of artists' work and pictures from magazines or even images from the internet. Using secondary sources is fine providing you are not copying someone else's work or idea. It is all in the development of the image and the interpretation.

It is important to keep 'playing' or experimenting. It is very easy for our work to get stale and for us to stay in a rut. If you have found a style that works for you it can be quite difficult to move on and develop new ideas. Working with a kit that has been created for you is fine every now and then but it is unlikely to develop your creative skills. Copying ideas from photographs can be a way forward, although it is always better to refer to and interpret your own photographs rather than someone else's.

Try going on workshops with a new tutor. While I obviously have a vested interest in promoting tutors, being one myself, I think we can make a big difference when a student is floundering and needs new ideas. I attend a five-day summer school every year to stretch myself and my creativity. I find it invaluable to work out of my comfort zone. How else can you develop new ideas and new techniques if you keep on working in the same old ways? While books are very important there is no substitute for working with an inspirational tutor along with a group of like-minded students. Not only do you learn from the tutor, you also benefit from everything the other students do.

It is important to remember that there are no mistakes.

Cut paper – counterchange

This exercise can be used as the whole design or can be used to take a section (for more on this, see page 25).

For this exercise you will need:

- One piece of black paper
- A piece of white paper twice the size of the black paper
- Scissors or a scalpel
- Cutting mat
- Glue

One of the simplest ways of creating designs is to use cut or torn papers. I was lucky enough to be given some wonderful books by my tutor Maeve Edwards when she gave up teaching. One of them was *Creative Paper Cutting* by Ernst Rottger. It is still available second-hand and is very inspiring. This is a simple exercise that can be done on your own or in a group; try to take some time over it and you will reap the benefits.

Take a piece of black paper. It can be any shape but a square or rectangle is easier to start with. Cut several shapes into the side of the paper. Flip the shapes out like opening a door, making sure to keep the edges of the paper in line. Once you have cut your shapes, stick them down carefully onto a white sheet of paper. You will find the white sheet of paper will need to be at least twice the size of the black piece. Cutting with scissors does not allow for very complicated shapes unless you are very patient, so I recommend using a scalpel and cutting mat. You will have much more control over the shape you cut. Always be very careful when using scalpels, as the slightest mistake can lead to bloodshed. Make sure you keep the blade covered when not in use. A cork will make a good cover if you do not have a retractable blade on your scalpel.

Once you have tried a straight-sided shape, experiment with a circle or several strips of varying widths.

Above: Cut paper exercise using a scalpel and cutting mat by Kim Thittichai.

'The Journey'

This exercise is particularly good for people working in groups; create the mood by putting some music on in the background and let your minds wander. For this exercise you will need:

- One sheet of white A1 paper
- Watered-down black acrylic paint
- At least five brushes of different sizes
- Masking tape

Fold the paper in half longways and cut or tear apart. Tape two of the short sides together so you have a very long piece of paper. Changing the size and proportions of the paper you work on changes the way you move and the marks that you make.

When I do this absorbing exercise with a group of students I get them to do some limbering-up stretches first: relax your shoulders, stretch your arms towards the ceiling, stretch your arms to the side and 'draw' large circles in the air. All this will help you make larger, more flowing marks and it also helps to break the ice. It can be very intimidating to be asked to draw in front of other people. It is important to emphasize that this is a mark-making exercise not a painting competition.

Paint a journey; it could be the journey taking the children to school, it could be an imaginary walk in a mythical forest or somewhere you have been on holiday. It doesn't really matter what it is. Half of the fun of this exercise is the play-school quality of it. We are all so busy rushing around in our busy lives; we rarely take the time out to take a line for a walk. Use as many widths of brush as you can find. This will help your drawing look more interesting and will help when you are isolating designs at a later stage (see page 25).

Below: The Journey, an exercise painted by Jane Potter. Working on a very wide format — or any other unusual shape — encourages you to think out of the box.

If you have large open areas of space on your 'journey', try filling them in with different shapes, spots, stripes and squiggles – whatever you fancy. Work these areas instinctively – let your hand do the thinking. When you have finished your journey and it is dry, try hanging it on the wall long ways down, as shown left. It will look quite different.

If you are working in a group it looks amazing when you hang several together.

Left: A selection of exercises hung side by side to create a larger design.

Below: 'The Journey', an exercise painted by Frances Davis.

2   using 3"x 3" window, choose 10 sections for future designs, balancing heavy lines and shapes with areas of more intricate detail.

Large-scale still life

Yes, I know the term 'still life' fills most people with dread but it is possible to have fun with this kind of exercise. It is particularly successful when working in a group as you can all contribute to the still life. Again, it is very important to stress that this is not a painting or drawing competition.

When I was teaching my third- and fourth-year students we were lucky enough to have access to the art room at college. It was a lovely old, long room with wooden floors and tall windows that let in plenty of light, the kind of room that all the art and craft tutors fought over. We would line up tables down the length of the room and then set up the still life. This would include chairs, massive plants, vases, anything large scale we could find. The students then added anything they had brought in, from brightly patterned scarves and parasols to a teddy bear – something that they thought would be interesting to draw. The easels and drawing boards were then lined up and the students decided where they wanted to stand or sit to draw and paint. We used lining paper for most of the exercises as it is cheap and can be of any length. We started off with a big, wet and splashy painting around 1.5m (5ft) long.

The impression of what the students were looking at was what I was after, not a strict representation. It was important that they really looked at what was in front of them – where two lines crossed and where there were spaces that were created in between. A curve had to be a proper curve, not just a wiggle. The students were encouraged to make confident marks and not worry too much about what they looked like. Some incredible work was produced. As we had the whole day, many paintings and sketches were made, some taking just five minutes and some taking an hour. We used paints, crayons, pastels and drawing pencils. All were used for taking sections and discovering new colour combinations.

Why not have a go yourself. Suggest it to your group and you might be pleasantly surprised at what you produce. If you don't try, you will never know what you can do...

Below: Students on the Experimental Textiles course, painting sections of a large still life.

Taking a section

Taking sections of your work and isolating designs can generate some very pleasing and totally original work. You just need two L-shapes of card or paper. You can also use a window mount but L-shapes are more versatile as they can be moved up and down and in and out. If you have done any of the previous exercises you will have plenty of chances to try this out. If not, try it on a photograph or drawing you already have.

Take the L-shapes and arrange them on your work to make a square 'window'. Keep moving the L-shapes over your work until you find a pleasing design. This can then be traced onto tracing paper and kept for use later. It is possible to create many designs from just one exercise. Try varying the shapes: long thin ones, wide ones, triangles. Just play and see what happens, and remember to try turning your work sideways or upside down, as Frances did for her sample, above; again it is the old issue of time that can spoil this kind of exercise. If you can allow yourself to spend time on this you will have a book full of original designs in an afternoon. It is important to work only in black and white at this stage as colour can be very distracting and you need to concentrate purely on the design.

Above: A section has been taken from 'The Journey' exercise on the previous page, enlarged and interpreted in fabric by Frances Davis. Sometimes students also annotate their sketchbooks with notes on materials and techniques used.

Below: A section taken with L-shapes of card.

Starting to develop your designs

This section taken from Jane Potter's sketchbook (see pages 20–21) was enlarged on the photocopier and then interpreted as a simple appliqué. Parts of the original design were left out to make the design easier to translate.

When you switch from paper to fabric to interpret a design there are many things to consider: fabric can fray where you need a hard edge, for example, and how do you create a spotty effect? What looks like a very simple exercise can become quite a brain teaser, but that is how you learn.

Above: The pages of this sketchbook demonstrate the variety of designs that Jane has created from her 'Journey' (see page 20–21).

Right: One section from the left-hand column of the above sketchbook, enlarged and interpreted in fabric and thread by Jane Potter. Black cotton fabrics and yarn have been cut and stitched to interpret the section. Note that areas of the original drawing have been left out to give a clearer design.

Developing Your Designs and Ideas

So now you have a book full of lovely designs, how do you develop them? One way is to create your own printing blocks. This easy way came from one of Ruth Issett's summer schools. It has been invaluable to me and to my students. There are more printing block ideas in Ruth's book, *Print, Pattern and Colour* (see Further Reading, page 126).

Making your printing blocks is a great way to make your work unique. There are many different ways to construct blocks. They can be carved from one piece of wood or rubber or can be made from many single items stuck to a firm background. The printing surface can be created from anything from string to can lids. As long as the surface is of a uniform height with no item higher than another you will create smooth prints. There is a wide choice of paints and dyes that can be used with printing blocks – even disperse dyes (transfer paints) can be thickened and printed with. All the work featured in this chapter has been embellished with printing blocks made by students from either the 'Journey' exercise (see page 20) or designing to music (see page 40).

Left: Sketchbook by Helen Igo showing prints made using her printing blocks.

A simple printing block

The materials required for making a simple printing block are:

- Foam-core board
- Scalpel
- Cutting mat
- Ruler
- A4 self-adhesive foam sheet in a pale colour
- Pencil

Measure the dimensions of your design and cut two pieces of the foam-core board to the same size. Cut one piece of self-adhesive foam to the same size. Transfer your design onto both sheets of foam-core board and the sheet of self-adhesive foam. The easiest way to do this is to press hard with a pencil and impress the design into the board and the foam and then go over the lines to make them more visible.

Place your self-adhesive foam onto your cutting mat and carefully cut out your design. Only cut where there are lines. Once you have completed cutting the whole design leave it on the mat and place the two pieces of foam-core board close by. Very carefully lift the design out of the foam and remove the backing paper. Stick this down onto one of your pieces of board. As you have already drawn your design onto the board you should have no problem seeing where to place your foam. The shape that is left on your cutting mat can then be stuck to the second piece of board.

You will then have the positive and negative parts of your design. It is important to remember that these blocks are not particularly washable but can be cleaned with baby wipes. Do not immerse them in water.

Now the fun can begin.

Your blocks can be used to print onto anything flat and you can use any printing medium that is the right consistency. I tend to use acrylics but they dry very quickly and you need to clean your blocks frequently to keep the designs clear. If you need any more information on printing media there is plenty of information in any book by Ruth Issett, particularly *Print, Pattern and Colour* (see Further Reading, page 126).

Right: Sketchbook belonging to Gwenda Baker showing traced sections of her Journey project, which were then used to create the printing blocks.

Below left and below right: Two print blocks created from one of the sections from Gwenda Baker's sketchbook.

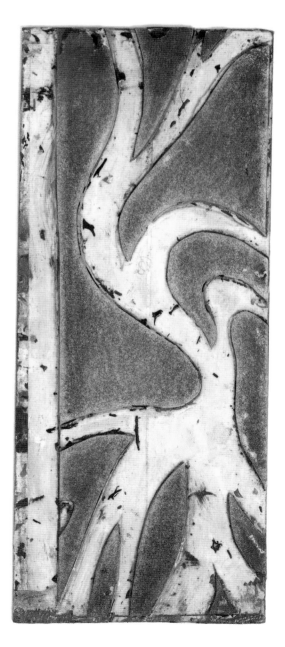

When you are working on a project do not just settle for the first colour combination that comes to mind – experiment.

If you have not used printing blocks before it is a good idea to experiment with different types of printing media. You need to get accustomed to the correct consistency that you need to coat your block and produce prints that are not too thick and gloopy.

Experiment with repeat designs and different coloured papers. If you are printing with acrylic onto white paper, try painting the paper with a wash of Procion dye once the acrylic is dry. The paint will resist the dye and you will have a more unusual and colourful print.

Try printing and dying papers in similar colour tones, tear them up and overlap and layer them to create interesting textures (see pages 34 and 49).

Once you are confidently printing onto paper try printing on different types of fabric, such as rough hessian and burlap, fine, smooth cottons and silks. Do you like the effect of printing onto creased fabric? Try stitching onto your fabric then printing over it (see next page).

Right: Getting to know your blocks.
Print by Gwenda Baker, washed with a
dilute mix of Procion dye powder.

Left: Torn and layered paper exercise by Gwenda Baker using hand-printed and torn papers.

Right: A similar exercise but this time using hand-printed and dyed fabric by Gwenda Baker.

'Bonfire' – Bea Taylor

These printing blocks were created by Bea Taylor for her project based on a bonfire of leaves. The finished piece incorporates printed and dyed cottons and linens. The leaves were then machine stitched to the backing fabric.

Left: Detail of 'Bonfire' (shown opposite), showing the different fabrics used for the leaves.

Below: The two print blocks used for this project were created by Bea Taylor from foam, double-sided tape and foam core board.

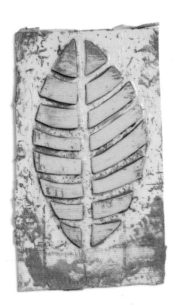

Left: 'Bonfire' by Bea Taylor. The leaves were printed onto different fabrics then cut out and appliquéd in place.

'Blue Panel' — Helen Igo

Every second-year student was asked to create a 120 × 30cm (4 × 1ft) panel for their end-of-year show; it was always fascinating to see how, with the same brief, they all created something different. Helen Igo started by making her printing blocks, then dying some calico. She decided to leave the creases in for added texture. Helen then cut 13 sections of dyed calico the same size and printed them with the same block. The sections were then embellished with silver thread.

Helen's sketchbooks are a joy to behold with well-considered samples and plenty of written-up ideas for future work.

Below: Detail of 'Blue Panel' showing the printed sections on the spaced-dyed calico.

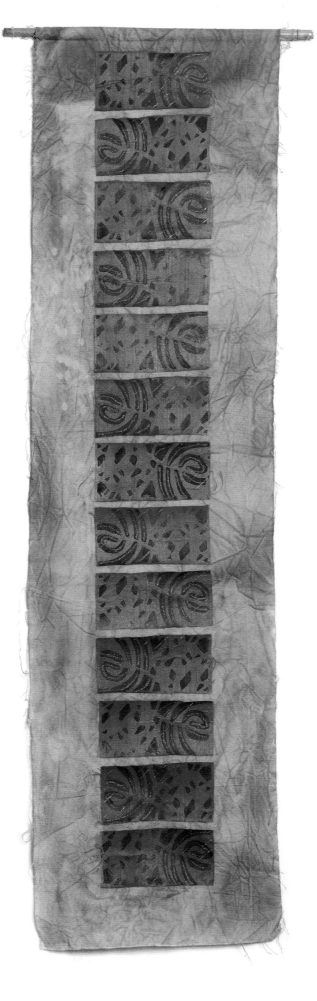

Left: 'Blue Panel' by Helen Igo.

Below: Part of Helen's sketchbook showing the printing block she used for this piece of work.

Red flower panel – Karen Cunningham

The following pages show the whole journey from inspiration to finished piece.
This 120 × 30cm (4 × 1ft) panel was also produced by a second-year student.

After 'The Journey' project undertaken in the first year, in the second year we did something similar with the theme of music. Three different types of music are played and the students make marks to all three types in black on white. They then change to colour and see what each piece of music evokes. Not only does the student have plenty of reference from which to take sections, they also have a ready-made colour scheme.

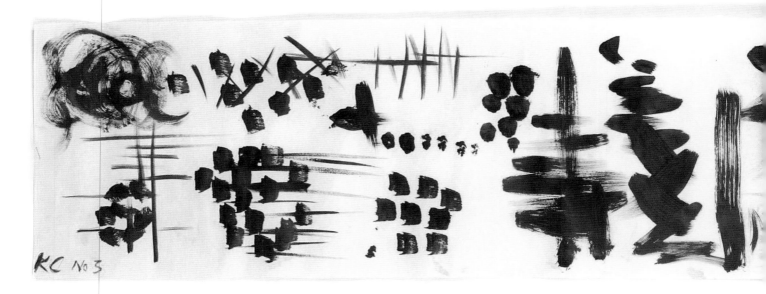

Below: Karen's first try at painting the music.

Bottom: Karen chose the piece of music 'Te Deum' by Charpentier for her panel. These are the colours and regular marks that the music inspired.

Left and below: These printing blocks were created by tracing sections of the paper exercise on the previous page.

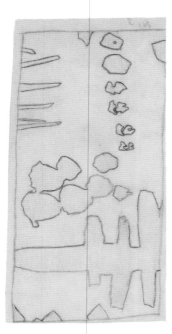

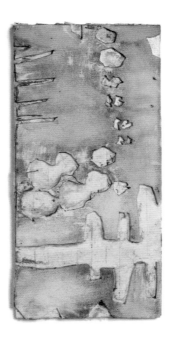

These printing blocks have been created by tracing areas from the music panel shown on the previous page.

Try printing on different coloured papers, often changing the colours of printing media to build a library of prints.

Once Karen Cunningham had chosen which designs to use she began to experiment with different layering techniques to get the exact effect she required.

When she had finished sampling Karen had decided which fabrics to use. Polyester satin was printed on as the base fabric and then various layers were printed and layered on top. A final layer of applied fabrics was added to give definition (see page 45).

Below: Sample showing a three-tone print on black paper.

Left: A two-tone print, made with one of the blocks shown on page 42, on black paper.

Right: The first of several samples that Karen made to help her decide which techniques and processes to use on her panel. This sample is made from printed polyester satin, overlaid with printed and cut polyester organza.

There are many excellent books available on the use of colour and design (there are some suggestions at the back of this book) and it is not my intention to cover these subjects in any great detail here; I merely wish to encourage you to start a sketchbook and generate ideas that you will hopefully develop in the future.

When developing your ideas, remember that work can be simple, and that what you leave out can be as important as what you put in. Think of your idea as a piece of music – do you want the full orchestra playing or just a harmonious quartet? Do not throw everything you know at one piece of work – be selective.

Another thing to remember is that your original idea is likely to change and develop as you progress. This is natural and should not cause a problem unless you are working to a set commission.

Do not try to do everything at once, as the journey of the learning process is important and not to be hurried. No matter how many times you have worked with a process or technique it is sometimes surprising to discover you have learned something new. It could be something as subtle as the pressure you use with a print roller or the realization that you have been using the wrong tension on a sewing machine for years, which is why your thread always breaks. Just because you do something over and over again does not devalue the process.

Right: The finished panel.

Opposite: Detail of the finished panel showing layers of printed polyester organza, painted Bondaweb and appliqué.

Colour in Textiles

The use of colour should ideally be spontaneous. The rigid application of colour theory can tend to produce a predictable result. Colour has vitality and decorative power, it can create atmosphere, establish mood and evoke a strong emotional response.

A basic knowledge of colour principles helps in planning a colour scheme where there will be repeat patterns or the item has to co-ordinate with other things as in interior decoration or garden design. Theory also helps if a colour scheme is not working and needs rectifying.

When thinking about colour for use in textiles there are two basic categories to consider – emotion and information.

Emotion

Colour in art or design can be a means of expressing emotions or seeing the world in a different way. It can be an expressive response to what we see. The eye moves constantly, all the time taking in visual information. Colour is described by such words as strong, weak, bright, dull, hot, cold, depressing, exhilarating, subtle, aggressive, sophisticated, natural, artificial and so on.

A person's reaction to colour depends very much on their mood, health, age, sex, temperament, status or country they are in. The quality of sunlight where they live may also have a lasting effect on their colour preference. Outgoing people may like reds and yellows; tranquil people the blues and greens. Younger people may enjoy light, clear colours and older people the softer, subtler variations.

The ability of colour to alter people's moods and create atmosphere has long been known and used by interior designers. For example, orange or red seats and tables in restaurants make customers restless and encourage them not to linger, yet when orange is worn next to the skin it is emotionally healing. Pale pink is used in police cells to calm down violent inmates. Art therapists use colour to help diagnose mental illness. Try to think of how colour is used around you.

Information

The colour of objects tells us a lot about them. We use it to determine whether food is ripe or decaying; whether traffic lights are stop or go. It also helps to distinguish between shapes that are the same. Camouflage is used in the opposite way by breaking up a shape into bold areas of colour; the overall shape is harder to distinguish, or can be made to blend into the background.

Brand colours – Kodak's yellow, Cadbury's purple, national flags, uniforms, football strips, all act as ways to distinguish and identify groups or brands.

Right: Printed and torn papers by Lucy Spearman. There are many shocked faces in the room when you first ask students to tear up their work. Once they understand why, the students generally enjoy the exercise. What were several sheets of interesting printed experiments can become beautiful layered pieces of work that can be stitched into by hand or machine.

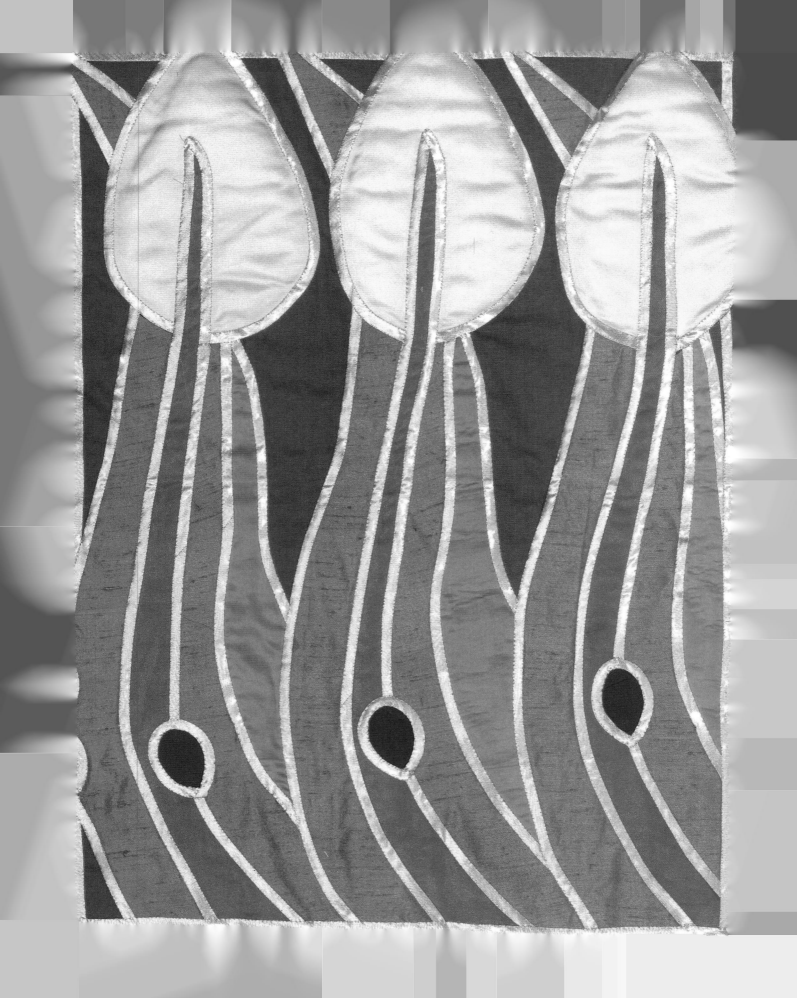

Physiological groupings

Feelings about colour are altered by association with the object. For example, red eyes look evil and frightening in a mask, but the same colour in a rose is thought to be beautiful and associated with love. Combinations of colour create an emotional response:

- **Dark cool:** mystery, melancholy. Dark blue suggests heaviness.
- **Light cool:** cold colours seem transparent and weightless. Light blue suggests delicacy, space, freshness, peace, hope.
- **Dark warm:** colours suggest richness, stability, power and energy.
- **Light warm:** creams and pinks, suggest femininity, youth and delight.
- **Bright warm:** colours suggest strong sunlight.

When you are next wandering around the supermarket trying to decide what to cook for dinner, have a look at some packaging and see if you can decide whom the product is aimed at by the colours used on the packaging. Certain alcoholic drinks will be packaged to appeal to naughty young things, while sweets and chocolate manufacturers will use different colours to appeal to children rather than adults. What makes the packaging on 'healthy' biscuits look different to others? The answer is colour! Why not try a group project to see how colours are used. Start with washing powder, chocolate and 'healthy' ready meals. You may be surprised by what you find.

Describing colour

Colour is described in the following terms:

- **Value:** the quality of light that a colour reflects. Light determines colour. Facing the light, objects look lighter (higher value) – facing away, they look darker (lower value).
- **Hue:** is the description of a colour – the brightest pure colour from the spectrum or colour wheel. It is what distinguishes red from orange or blue. It does not include black, white or grey.
- **Intensity:** strong or weak colour. The purity of the pigment determines its intensity, brightness or dullness. For example, coloured pencils have a lot of binder mixed in and so don't appear as intense as, say, oil; water-soluble pencils increase in intensity when a wash is added.
- **Tint:** white added to a hue gives a colour a higher value.
- **Tone:** grey added to a hue gives a duller colour. The lightest colour tonally is yellow. Red and green are mid tones; brown, purple and indigo are dark tones. In embroidery tone can be altered by changing direction of thread or grain of fabric. (The angle of the falling light gives highlights and shadows.)
- **Shade:** black added to a hue gives a lower value.
- **Black:** a mix of equal quantities of all colours gives black.
- **Brown:** a mix of equal quantities of red, yellow and blue (the primaries).

Most art and craft shops sell colour wheels that rotate to give many colour combinations and are very useful tools when trying to decide on a colour palette for a piece of work. However they are no substitute for mixing your own colours to create a colour wheel. It becomes more interesting when you try different media, such as paint, coloured tissue paper, chalk pastels and so on.

Opposite: 'Tulips', a small quilt by Josephine Milligan. This quilt caught my eye at the Creative Stitches show in Glasgow. It was one of several stained-glass quilts and the only one not to use a black as the outline for the pieces. By using gold bias strips, Josephine has created a much softer image yet still maintains definition.

The colour system

Primary   Yellow, red, blue

Secondary

Orange = Red + Yellow
Green = Blue + Yellow
Violet = Blue + Red

Tertiary

These colours are made by mixing each primary with the adjacent secondaries:
Red-Orange
Yellow-Orange
Yellow-Green
Blue-Green
Blue-Violet
Red-Violet

Below and right: These worksheets show colours mixed by Frances Davies.

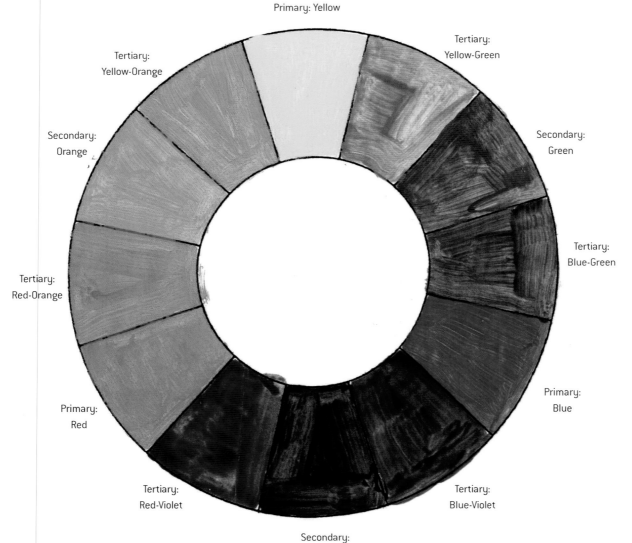

Primary: Yellow

Tertiary: Yellow-Green

Tertiary: Yellow-Orange

Secondary: Green

Secondary: Orange

Tertiary: Blue-Green

Tertiary: Red-Orange

Primary: Blue

Primary: Red

Tertiary: Red-Violet

Tertiary: Blue-Violet

Secondary: Violet

Colours from the colour wheel	Add white to make tints	Add black to make shades	Add complementary colour for muted hues
Primary: Yellow			
Tertiary: Yellow-Green			
Secondary: Green			
Tertiary: Blue-Green			
Primary: Blue			
Tertiary: Blue-Violet			
Secondary: Violet			
Tertiary: Red-Violet			
Primary: Red			
Tertiary: Red-Orange			
Secondary: Orange			
Tertiary: Yellow-Orange			

Complementary colours

Any two colours that are exactly opposite on the colour wheel are complementary. If complementary colours are used in very small areas of equal size, the effect will become greyed or brown from a distance. In medium to large amounts, complementary colours placed next to each other make each other look stronger and more vibrant.

When complementary colours are mixed together they make grey. If you are using pure pigment they will make black (in other words the mix contains all the colours).

Analogous colours

Analogous colours are two or three colours next to each other on the colour wheel, such as red and orange. They create a warm or cool effect.

Harmony

Order pleases the brain. The human eye and brain insist on grouping colour sensations together in a few wavebands. Therefore some groupings of colour will be more pleasing than others. Discord can be deliberately used to attract attention or give a warning.

Triad harmony
Refers to any three colours that are equidistant from each other on the colour wheel.

Monochromatic harmony
This is a colour scheme based on one colour but varying tints, tones, shades and textures.

Analogous harmony
This is a colour scheme using three to five colours that are next to each other on the colour wheel, such as blues and greens for example.

Split complementary
This is a scheme using the colours either side of the hue, plus the complementary. For example, red-violet plus red-orange and green (the complementary of red). The effect is strong but less aggressive than true complementaries.

Mutual complementary
This refers to five analogous colours with the complementary of the central colour.

When you mix your colours you create new and exciting hues, so try to resist using your dyes and paints straight from the pot or tube. Your work will be much more interesting and have greater depth if you mix some of them.

Exercise

In your sketchbook create a rough line using each of these harmonies. Try using colours you see in advertisements and in articles in magazines.

- Analogous harmony
- Split complementary
- Mutual complementary
- Triad harmony

Below: A sketchbook showing pages that are Procion dyed in monochromatic harmony.

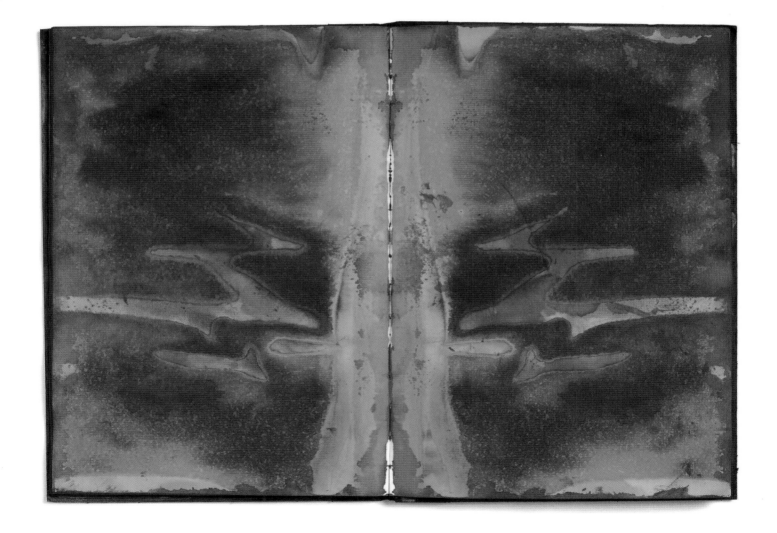

Part Two

Choosing Your Subject

Divine inspiration rarely strikes when you need it most so it is important to keep notes of any ideas you may have, when you have them. This selection of work has been chosen because the ideas came from students' scrapbooks and sketchbooks.

'The Ladies' — Morna McGibbon

Choosing your subject out of nowhere is very difficult. There are ways to get round this and one way is to go the sampler route, as followed by Morna McGibbon.

Morna had bought a small wooden Madonna icon while on holiday on the island of Lesbos, Greece. It was a simple design with carved lines as the only decoration. Morna started to make samples thinking she would make one large, finished piece. However, as her samples developed she decided to use them all and create a sampler. Morna had originally thought of creating a repeated image in the bright, colourful style of Andy Warhol but decided to go down a more traditional route. The techniques used include silk paper, melted plastic bags, English quilting, appliqué and monoprinting. It was important to limit the colour scheme otherwise the details would have been lost. The whole thing was brought together by using the same printed frame from a printing block that Morna had made. The heavy black cotton is a great contrast and holds all the separate pieces firmly in place.

Left: Detail of 'The Ladies' showing a simple monoprint.

Right: 'The Ladies' by Morna McGibbon. Various techniques are shown here, including melted plastic bags, English quilting, Trapunto and appliqué. The piece is 91 x 61cm (3 x 2ft)

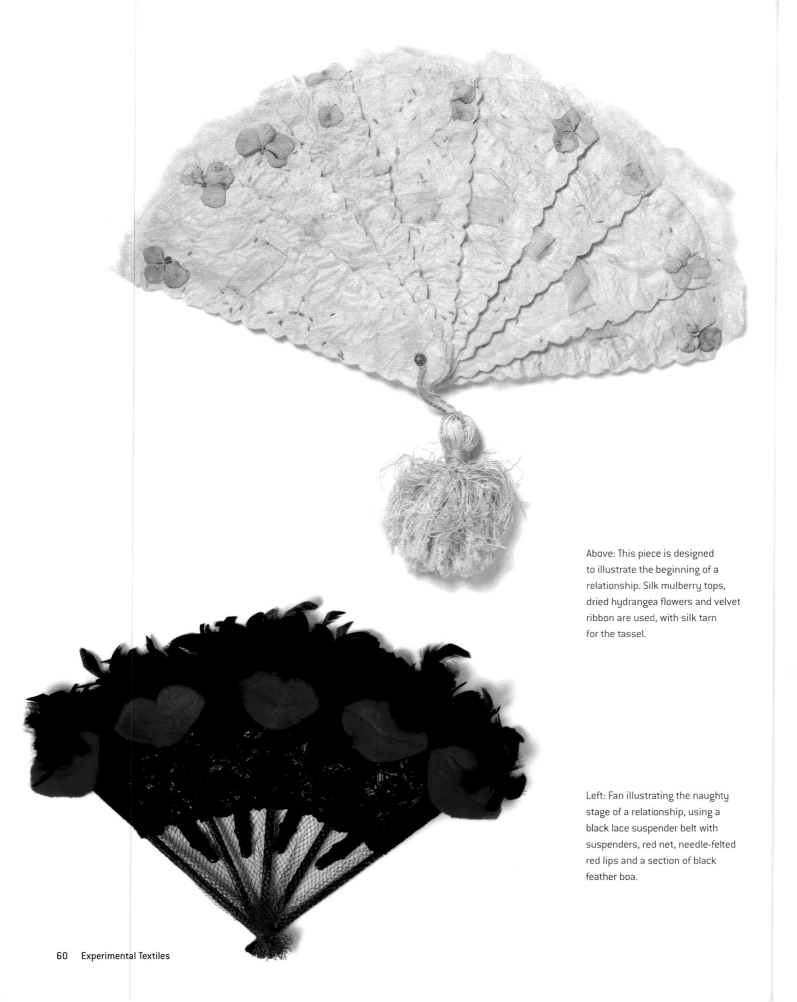

Above: This piece is designed to illustrate the beginning of a relationship. Silk mulberry tops, dried hydrangea flowers and velvet ribbon are used, with silk tarn for the tassel.

Left: Fan illustrating the naughty stage of a relationship, using a black lace suspender belt with suspenders, red net, needle-felted red lips and a section of black feather boa.

'Sevillanas' – Amanda Simmonds

Amanda Simmonds's project was based on the language of fans. Amanda had been attending a Flamenco class and had become increasingly fascinated with the whole culture of fans. She had learnt to dance the Sevillanas, a dance that incorporated the use of a fan and told the story of a romantic relationship. Amanda took this idea further by making four fans that told a similar story for her project:

- The first fan (shown left) describes the pure, romantic beginning of a relationship using soft natural colours, silk fibres and dried flowers.

- The second fan (below left) portrays the more physical side of the relationship when you know each other better and cannot keep your hands off each other.

- The next fan (below) is perfectly balanced in purple, describing the time when you are in harmony with your partner.

- The final fan (right) illustrates the breakdown of the relationship using heat-distressed synthetic fabrics.

Below: The end of a relationship is captured in this fan, using heat-distressed synthetic fibres that have been stitched and woven onto light struts to create the fan shape.

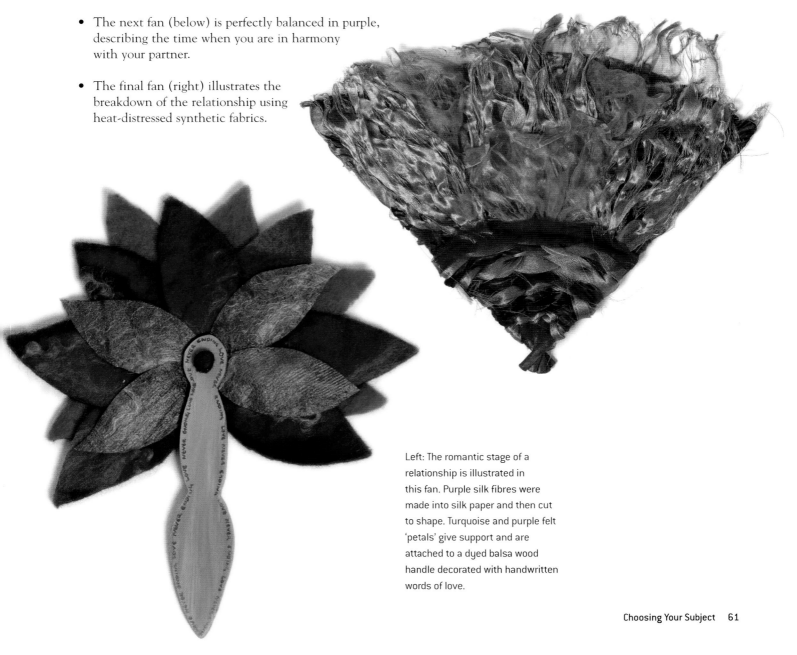

Left: The romantic stage of a relationship is illustrated in this fan. Purple silk fibres were made into silk paper and then cut to shape. Turquoise and purple felt 'petals' give support and are attached to a dyed balsa wood handle decorated with handwritten words of love.

Good taste or bad taste?

Are there any subjects that are taboo in textiles? It is interesting to consider this. Can any subject be deemed inappropriate? There seems to be no problem in the fine art field so theoretically there should be no such problem in the textile field. Because textile pieces are generally executed by women (though happily this is fast changing with many men taking up the textile challenge), it is sometimes seen as unseemly, particularly for women, to be seen to be inspired by an awful tragedy rather than a softer, more traditionally feminine subject.

'Ground Zero' (described below) and the Necrotext project (see pages 64–65) are two examples of work produced when difficult or sensitive issues are tackled using textiles.

'Ground Zero' – Eleanor Fielder

Eleanor Fielder felt so strongly about the disaster of 9/11 that she wanted to create a piece of work to illustrate it. Eleanor is not known for holding back on the embellishment of her work, which is usually very colourful and sparkly, but this was not going to be appropriate for such an emotive subject. A large book of newspaper cuttings was quickly created; there was plenty of choice at the time, from which Eleanor eventually found her image. Next she had to decide how to interpret it. The original work had fluffy clouds floating across the skeleton of the building. When the work was discussed by the group, they decided that the clouds made the piece look too 'pretty'; everyone thought it was important to keep the image stark.

In the final work the skeleton of the building was made from strips of balsa wood covered in hand-dyed silk velvet to give a soft, dusty effect. The bottom part of the work is a collage of newspaper photographs that has been transferred to the background with Image Maker, a liquid that makes lovely thick images that can be stitched and scratched into. Image Maker can be rather laborious to use but when it works it is excellent. The only stitching in the work is fine hand stitch on the helmets of the rescue workers and the stars and stripes flag. The background is space-dyed linen.

Right: 'Ground Zero' by Eleanor Fielder. This piece was kept deliberately stark to capture the shock of the events in New York on September 11th, 2001.

Group project – Necrotex

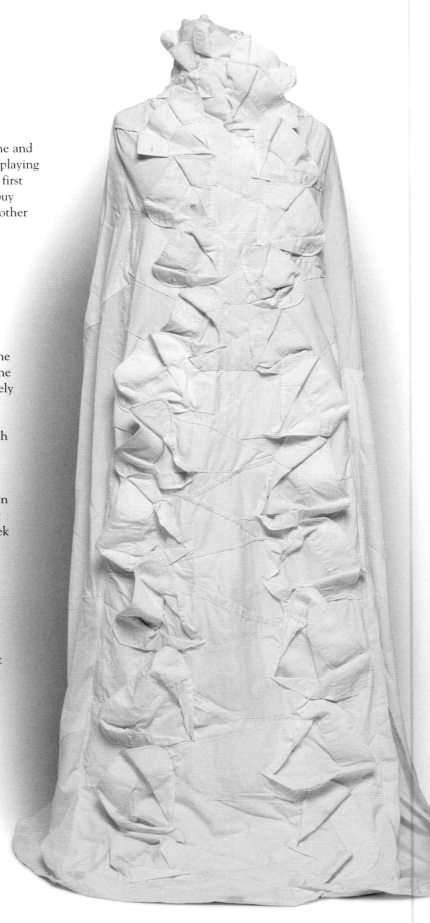

The next project began as a simple conversation in the classroom. One student, Helen Fallowfield, mentioned she and her mother had passed a shop called Arca, which was displaying a papier-mâché coffin in the widow. Arca was one of the first shops where you could organize a humanist funeral and buy coffins that were totally biodegradable. Helen and her mother discussed the pros and cons of this kind of burial. Helen thought it was a very good idea, but her mother was less keen. In fact when her mother got home she booked her own traditional funeral; pine coffin with brass handles and all.

The group started to discuss funerals in general then went on to talk about how they would like their funerals arranged, down to the music they wanted played, what the guests should wear and the kind of food to be served at the party afterwards. All the students agreed it would definitely have to be a party.

We then began to talk about traditions for handling death around the world. We discussed the Mexican Day of the Dead and the huge coffins seen in Africa. We started to talk about what we would like to wear when we were buried or cremated. I mentioned that I would like to lie in an open coffin as I would love to make myself something fantastic to wear, such as a heavily textured, layered Tyvek shroud studded with gems with a small ruffle-type collar and maybe even a headdress. The students all went off into the realms of fantasy describing all the wonderful outfits they would create for themselves.

It suddenly hit me; this would make a fantastic exhibition. But was it possible? Would anyone come and look at the exhibition when they realized the subject matter? I asked the group what they thought and they all thought it might work. By the end of the lesson we had decide on the name 'Necrotex' and decided we would make the Necrotex exhibition one of our projects.

What started as a fight of fancy soon took hold and the finished Necrotex project included objects from denim coffins to silk-paper death masks.

There had been a big discussion as to how we were to promote the exhibition; we did not want to use the shock factor. We were aware that people would come in and then possibly be upset by the content – death is not the usual subject for a textiles show. It was decided that some kind of quiet area should be set aside with tables and chairs and cake on offer, where people could sit and chat to the students if they wished, maybe even talk about someone they had lost. This would be another opportunity for many of my students to shine, as they were wonderful cake makers.

Interest in the exhibition escalated in a remarkable fashion. The BBC came and interviewed two of the students and this, along with pictures of the exhibition, was put on the BBC's website. Necrotex then toured with the Creative Stitches shows run by International Craft and Hobby Fairs to Brighton Centre, Birmingham NEC and Fashion and Embroidery at Harrogate. There have been several more airings of the exhibition and future dates have been suggested.

This group of students is still exhibiting together as 'Angelico'. Website details for this group and other students are at the back of the book.

Opposite: 'Shroud' by Hazel Imbert. Hazel used the shirts of the men in her family to create this life-sized piece. The shroud is designed so that Hazel can have the arms wrapped around her when she is buried.

Below: The collars of the shirts used to make 'Shroud' (shown opposite) were used to create this vessel. Hazel has written in indelible pen the loving messages and wishes she would like to leave to her children.

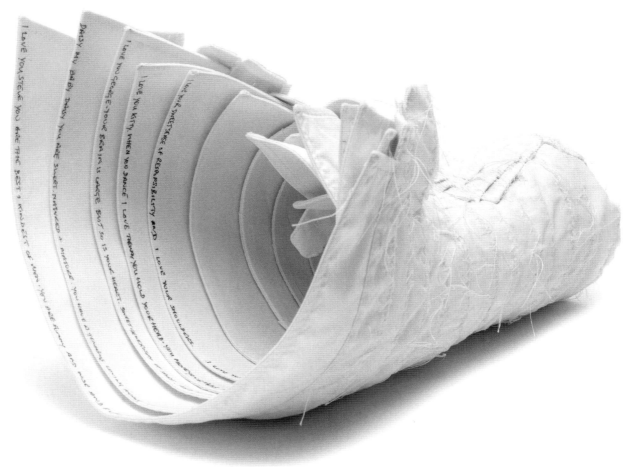

Interpretation

The way you interpret and express your ideas is totally personal to you. I have found it is best to try to keep things simple and not throw every technique you know at your piece of work. If you have a strong idea you don't need to impress with complicated layers of whatever is fashionable at the time – let the materials and processes you choose do the work. (As in all things there are exceptions that prove the rule – see Nikki Parmenter's work on scale on page 96.) It is generally good practise to make samples to try out your ideas before you launch into your finished piece of work; however, it is possible to 'wear out' your idea. You need to keep some energy back for the final work.

'Body Dresses' – Jaynie Rawling

Jaynie Rawling's work has always been concerned with labour-intensive materials, deterioration and disintegration of surfaces. She is also fascinated by the interaction between the second and third dimensions. The question of longevity and impermanence is integral to the rusty 'Body Dresses' that she constructs. Forever changing and breaking down as time takes its toll, the sculptural forms gradually metamorphose to reveal their fragility.

The juxtaposition of strength and weakness is underlined by the materials she uses; at first glance they appear to be heavy, distressed metals but they are actually lightweight, stitched and moulded Lutradur impregnated and treated with special paints and a heat gun. Many of Jaynie's larger pieces are extremely sculptural and can be suspended rather than free standing.

Lutradur is a spunbond polyester material that comes in four weights. Jaynie has used CS 800 (similar to Lutradur 130, the heaviest weight), which is strong enough for three-dimensional projects. Lutradur can be distressed with a heat gun for wonderful lacy effects. (For another example of this versatile material, see page 92.)

Jaynie is excited by the prospect of developing her work further. She is fascinated by a wide range of mediums, which provide a lot of scope for manipulation and experimentation. Particularly intriguing are the types of material that require meticulous working underlined with some kind of alchemic process. An obsession with surface detail can occasionally be frustrating but it is an integral part of her working process. Jaynie's work is three-dimensional as she wishes to invite the viewer to study her pieces from all angles, from inside to out and from a distance and close up.

'Company Man' – Jill Flower

Jill Flower graduated as a mature student with distinction in Stitched Textile Art at the East Berkshire College/Buckingham New University in Windsor. She is a Licentiate of the Society of Designer Craftsmen.

Jill has an avid interest in stitched textiles that has spanned the past 20 years. Jill originally achieved City and Guilds Part I/II in 1995 and in 2003 was selected to exhibit a piece of her work, an elaborate and brightly coloured handbag, at the Victoria & Albert Museum in London. During her three-year college course Jill pursued an interest in edgings and researched the history of lace and its influences on fashion. For her final exhibition piece she conceived the idea of combining the formality of Elizabethan lacy ruffs with Shakespeare's speech on 'The Seven Ages of Man' from *As You Like It*. Jill developed the story and created three life-sized, light-hearted pieces to form a theatrical 'Trinity of Ruffs' – man, woman and child. It is a modern-day interpretation using a unique manipulation of stitch and scraps of printed matter trapped into a crusty, lace-like fabric.

Each 'age' is interpreted by the use of recycling pages from magazines depicting our influences, developments and interests as we mature. For example, she used sections from comics for schoolboys; girly magazines for young men/lovers; financial papers for businessmen through to weather reports and crosswords for retirement, finishing with the obituaries page! Similarly, the lady's ruff contains abstracts from glamour, careers, brides and housekeeping magazines.

From this large installation work came the 'Circle of Life' series. The series has the same witty concept and story but this time manipulated into three-dimensional pieces housed in beautiful perspex wall-mounted boxes. This series was selected to be part of the International Art of the Stitch Open Exhibition 2008/9, touring to Birmingham in the UK, Krefeld in Germany, Budapest in Hungary and Seville in Spain. Excitingly, the work was also shortlisted by the Royal Academy for their summer exhibition, which they said 'was a huge achievement' for a newcomer and textile artist.

Jill's latest collection is called the 'Celebration Series', making individual pieces celebrating special events such as christenings, anniversaries and special birthdays all from recycled papers. These are particularly popular as they can be personalized with relevant names and dates.

Jill enjoys continuing to research different techniques, pushing the boundaries of stitch with recycled papers. She has found it amusing playing with the magazines, their sensational headlines, scripts and colours, and takes pleasure in incorporating cheeky comments within her pieces. She is now experimenting with a miniature body of work, which she says is 'quite a test after being so theatrically flamboyant'.

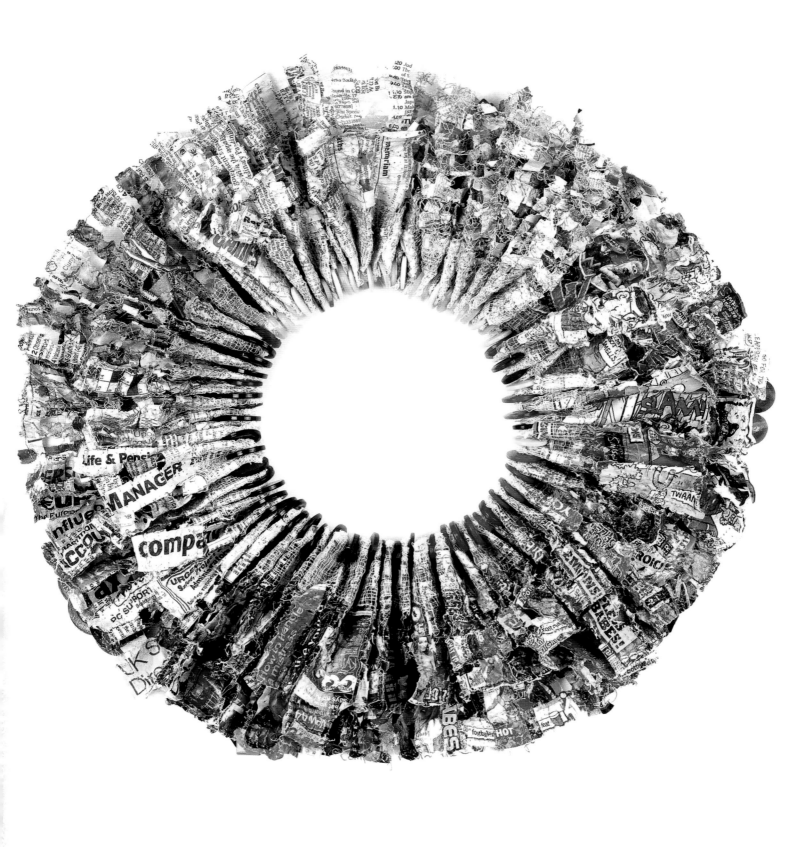

'Sunday Morning' from 'Sea Interlude' series

— Debbie Lyddon

Debbie Lyddon originally worked as a musician, playing and teaching the flute. Now as a textile artist she is combining two elements, drawing together two of the senses, sight and sound. In 'Sea Interlude' Debbie has explored ways of taking impressions of a piece of music and expressing visually the emotions and mood revealed to her.

For this body of work Debbie took Benjamin Britten's *Four Sea Interludes* as her inspiration. This piece of music consists of four movements entitled 'Dawn', 'Sunday Morning', 'Moonlight' and 'Storm'. The four movements inspired her to create one large narrative piece, approximately 650cm × 56cm (21ft × 22in) encompassing all four Interludes, and four smaller pieces, approximately 120cm × 50cm (4ft × 20in). 'Sunday Morning' is the second in this series.

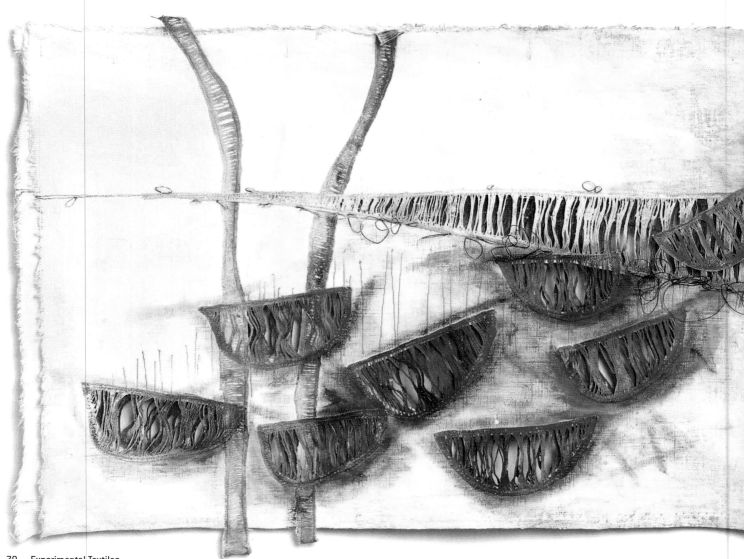

Britten's own annotations on his score furnish an insight into the composer's mind: seascape, slow wave, wind, gulls, spray blowing. These words were the basis of Debbie's interpretation and this context has enabled her to incorporate the two elements of music and seascape.

The north Norfolk coast has big skies, long sandy beaches and small muddy creeks, with boats moored on the banks, along which the tide seeps in and out. Debbie has combined her personal observations with the musical features of rhythm, melody, harmony and pitch to create a visual expression of the music. The two essential elements of this environment are the horizon and the features that dissect it. These lines have become fundamental to her drawing, the horizontal line depicting melody and the vertical, rhythm and time. The other musical elements, harmony and pitch, are expressed by her use of colour. While blue is the obvious colour choice for a seascape, different tones of this colour can convey distinct qualities. As Wassily Kandinsky said in *Concerning the Spiritual in Art*: 'In music blue is like a flute, a darker blue a cello; a still darker a thunderous double bass; and the darkest blue of all – the organ'.

Below: 'Sunday Morning' by Debbie Lyddon, a different slant on drawn thread work, embellished and stitched with polypropylene string, gesso and acrylic paint. The piece is 120cm x 50cm (4ft x 20in).

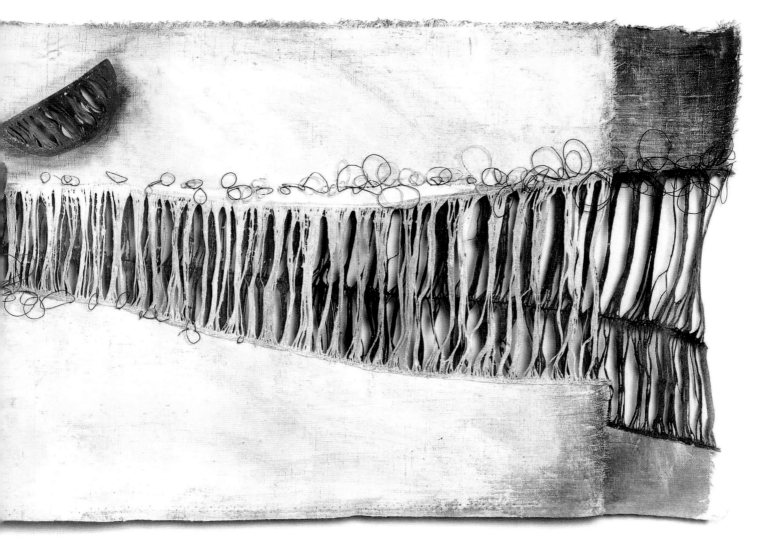

Personal observations of the landscape through drawing
are the foundation of this range of work. Debbie's aim is
to invoke rather than depict the landscape, using these
impressions as a support on which to hang musical
representation. She used simple materials; linen, loose-weave
linen, scrim, cotton thread, emulsion and acrylic paint.
Debbie had experimented with the technique of withdrawn
threads, challenging boundaries to create a textural surface
on which to paint. Found objects collected while walking on
the beach are used to embellish and springy polypropylene
ropes distressed by the sea have been used to stitch looped,
rhythmic and melodic lines that reveal themselves as the
eye is drawn along the canvas, in much the same way as
your ears hear music unfolding as it plays.

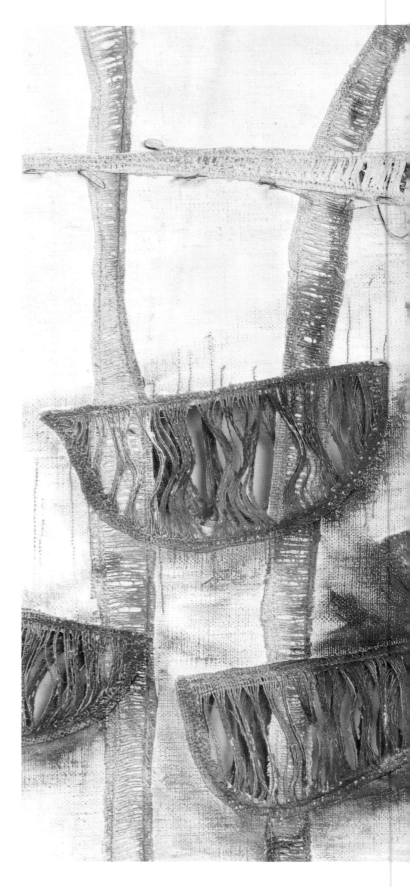

Right: Detail of 'Sunday Morning'
by Debbie Lyddon showing the
stitched details.

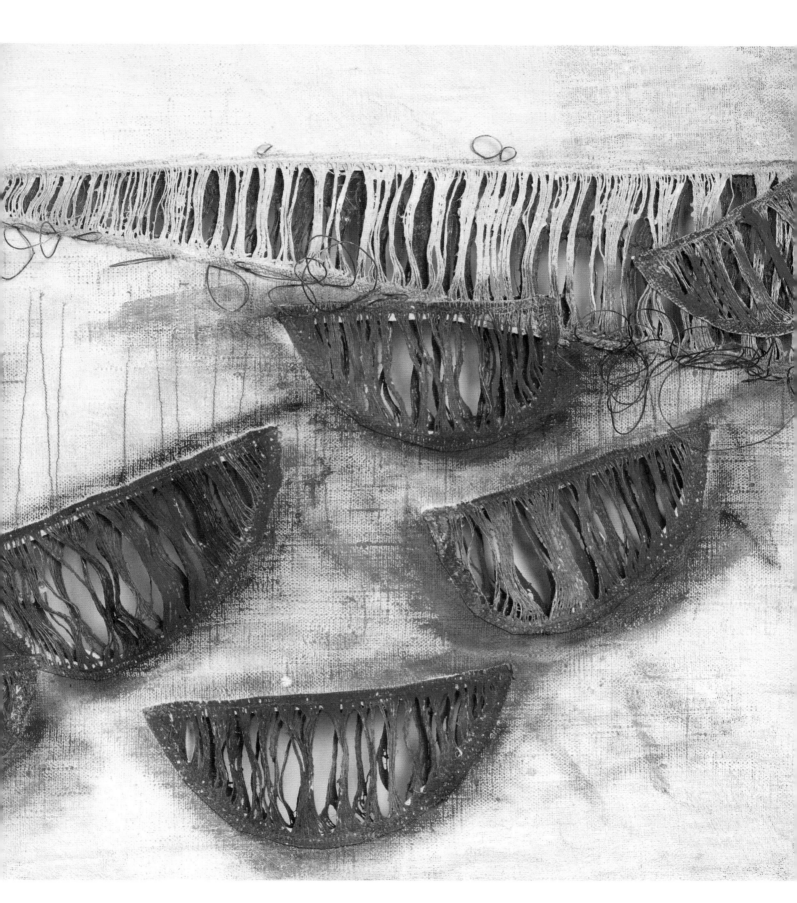

'Unveiled' — Liz Carter

'Threads' textile group, launched in September 2005, decided that the title of their first exhibition would be 'Unveiled'. After brainstorming for a while, perusing pictures and materials that I had encouraged the group to collect, Liz Carter was inspired by some pictures of fossilized waves and shells in her scrapbook, which were in black and white. After millions of years these amazing forms had been uncovered by a process of erosion, either by the weather or the sea. Liz sponge-printed the background colour on large panels of calico for both pieces.

For 'Fossilized Waves' (shown right), Liz gradually built up the design using a collection of fabrics and threads, reminiscent of the colours of stones on the beach at Crackington Haven, north Cornwall, manipulating the fabric strips and adding hand and machine stitch and beads.

'Fossilized Shells' (shown far right) needed a three-dimensional feel, so Liz decided to use padding and quilting to outline the fossil shells. More paint was applied to add highlights, and heavy machine whip stitch and cable stitch added to the crusty feel and merged the areas of colour. Green chiffon was added to knock back the brightness of the yellow paint, and to give a watery feel to the finished piece.

Right: 'Fossilized Waves' by Liz Carter showing heavy machine stitch, couching and space-dyed fabrics.

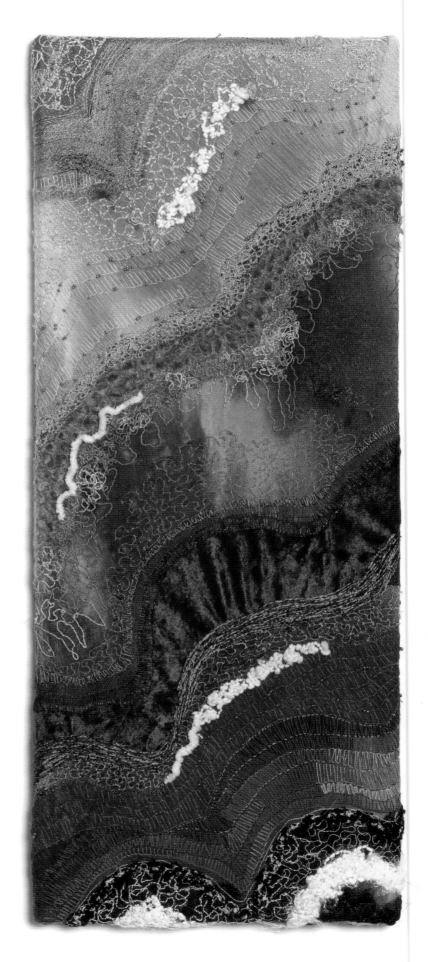

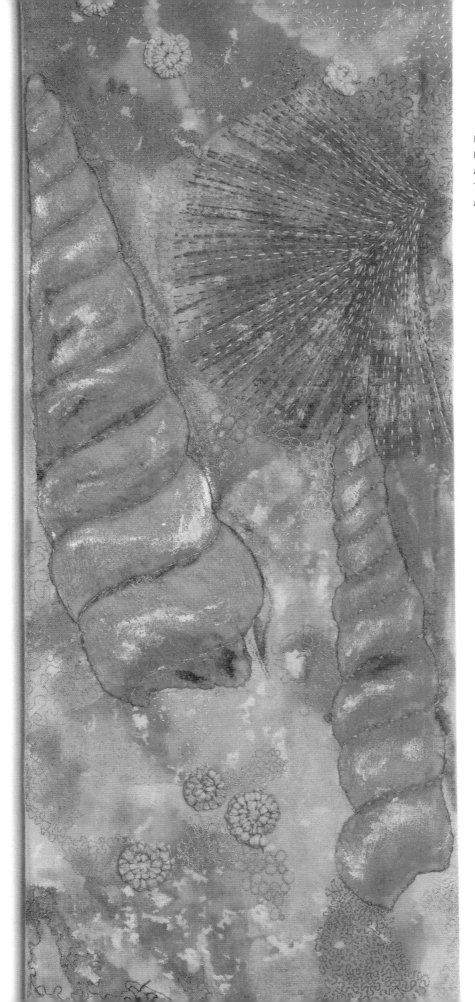

Left: 'Fossilized Shells' by Liz Carter showing hand and machine stitch, Trapunto quilting, couching and space-dyed fabrics.

'Avenue of Trees' — Jean Gerrard

This wall piece was Jean Gerrard's first-year project and a particular favourite of mine. Jean chose to photograph an avenue of trees at Nymans Gardens in West Sussex and work from that. I have a rule that students only work from drawings so Jean was encouraged to create her own sketch from the photograph. It can be too easy to snap away with a camera and not actually understand the angles, perspective and spaces between and around your subject. When you draw and start to look properly you will get a more accurate interpretation of your topic.

The photograph came in useful as it was difficult to sort out the light and dark in the image. So much colour in a picture can be distracting. We photocopied the photograph in black and white to get the tonal values that were necessary.

The floor of the avenue is rag rugged with cotton fabrics; the tree trunks are woven with wools, scrim and a little dark sparkly synthetic fabric. How to interpret the leaves and branches had us guessing for while but after a few experiments Jean settled on dyed silk filament for the branches and tiny pieces of cut-up silk paper for the leaves. The blue background is transfer-printed polyester satin.

Right: 'Avenue of Trees' by Jean Gerrard.

Left: Detail of 'Avenue of Trees' showing the rag-rugged floor of the avenue, the woven tree trunks and the silk paper leaves.

'Journeys by Train Through the Downs in Winter'

— Frances Davis

Frances Davies' weekly train journey could take up to an hour, and she began to notice more and more of her surroundings as she travelled. This piece was her interpretation of the journey she made through The Downs in Sussex each week. I was particularly pleased with the way Francis mounted the work to make it look like the reflections of the landscape through the windows of the train. The techniques used included English quilting, free machine embroidery, image transfer and hand stitch. Frances decided not to use colour in the work as she felt it would make a stronger impact in black and white.

Below and below right: The front and reverse sides of 'Journeys by Train Through the Downs in Winter' by Frances Davis.

Opposite: Detail showing image-transferred photographs of various landscapes with a running hand stitch to echo the rolling lines of the surrounding countryside.

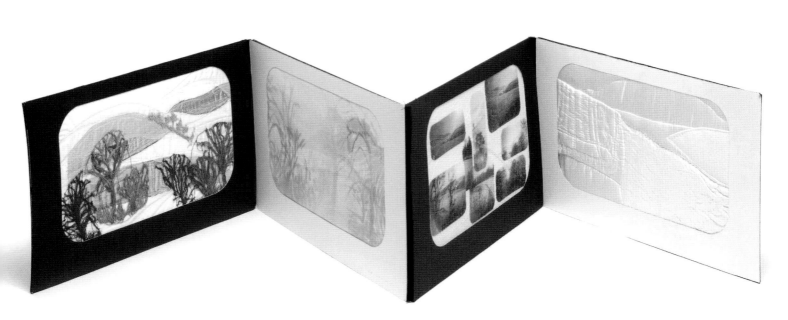

'Shoreline' — Jane Potter

'Shoreline' came about as a sample that developed into a finished piece. Sometimes when you are working it is best to carry on and develop the sample rather than finish it and then start again to make your finished piece. It is very easy to overwork your idea; the whole thing can become contrived rather than the fresh and exciting inspiration you had in the first place.

The class was set a two-week project on boundaries and edges. In the first week there was a class discussion during which a list of suggestions was made – incorporating metaphysical and physical and everyday expressions. Rather than using fabric the students were asked to use paper and the finished piece needed to measure at least 61cm (24in) on one side. We all brought every kind of paper we could find into the class and then the fun commenced. For this project the use of glue was not permitted.

Jane Potter's finished piece was one of the simplest but best considered. Her thoughts were on the shoreline near where she lives, where the breakwaters protrude unevenly from the sea and the walls hold back the sand dunes.

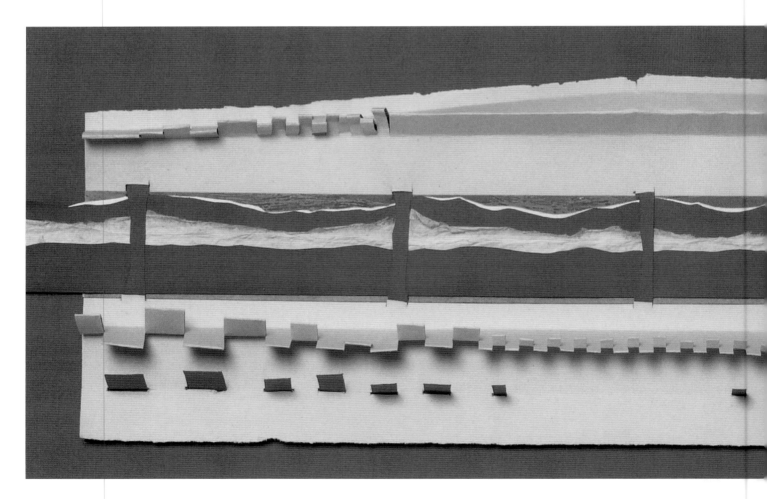

Below are a few suggestions of lines and edges; can you think of any more examples?

Barriers	Boundaries	Edges	Lines
Disability	Fences	Frayed	Equator
Poverty	Walls	Torn	Timelines
Health	Seas	Ripped	Ley lines
Geography	Rivers	Curled	Borders
Time	Roads	Burnt	Horizon
Age		Cut	Meridian
Education		Coast	Shipping lanes
Confidence		Crimp	
Skin		Smooth	
Technology		Rough	

Shoreline is constructed from a light brown/grey card and a dark cream sugar paper highlighted with a strip of hand-dyed cartridge paper and a natural textured handmade paper. A combination of cutting and tearing has formed an interesting set of edges that create beautiful shadows and therefore even more edges.

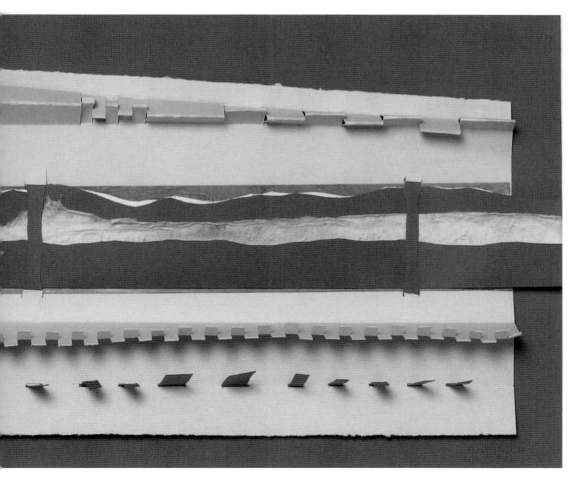

Left: 'Shoreline' by Jane Potter. Manipulated and torn papers folded and cut to represent the coast close to where Jane lives. The repeated, folded sections are reminiscent of the groynes that punctuate the coastline.

Three Dimensions

When working in three dimensions there are many things to consider. Does the material or media you are working with need some kind of reinforcement? Will you be needing a supporting framework or will you be using a firm material? The following seven artists have all been chosen for the different ways they approach this quandary.

'Ring' Casket & 'Gormanghast' — Carol Coleman

Having moved house around 30 times, Carol Coleman has a guiding principle of 'You can never have too many boxes.' She never makes samples, so she likes to test materials, colours, textures and techniques by making small boxes. It is relatively easy to produce something in two dimensions, but making a three-dimensional functional object from textiles or other soft material can be a bit of a challenge. Carol likes to see how far the chosen material can be manipulated and how big a structure she can make without using any supporting framework or card. Carol's favoured techniques involve free-machine embroidery and cold-water dissolving film, so all materials have to be colourfast and able to go through water. You must also be able to stitch through the materials without breaking needles or thread.

Carol says: 'The little Gothic fossil box, 'Gormanghast', was my first experiment with Softsculpt thermoplastic foam. I heated the foam and impressed it with ammonites, and after cutting out the six sides of the box, cut windows in the foam and layered some red crystal organza and green metallic fabric to show through the window and also to form the lining. I then mounted each panel on dissolving film and machine stitched the panels together one by one, making the fringing at the same time. I also impressed some little circles of foam and applied these separately along with some beads. The ammonite impressions gave me an indication of where I might like to stitch and the black colour of the foam and my choice of a dark metallic thread gives the box a rather Gothic feel.

The cling-film (plastic wrap) casket, 'Ring' casket, was made with the leftovers from my daughter's wedding accessories – freshwater pearls, citrine and rock crystal. I made cling-film "sandwiches" by layering small bits of pale cream thread and fabric between sheets of cling film and then lightly ironing them between sheets of baking parchment. I then lightly bonded some pale gold crystal organza to the back to give some strength and body and also to show through where the cling film was still clear. I wanted the inside of the box to be silver, so I then bonded some silver fabric on top of the organza. Using my templates, I then cut out each panel and worked and assembled them in the same way as the Gothic box.'

Right: 'Gormanghast' casket by Carol Coleman, constructed from thermoplastic foam, machine-embroidered lace and machine stitch with added bead embellishment.

Below: 'Ring' casket by Carol Coleman. Free-machine embroidered cling film (plastic wrap) decorated with freshwater pearls and crystals, embellished with machine-embroidered lace.

'Changing Landscape' — Wendy Dolan

Wendy Dolan is an experienced lecturer and tutor in creative textiles. She has exhibited widely in the UK and is a member of the Society of Designer Craftsmen and The Sussex Guild of Contemporary Designer Makers.

This three-dimensional vessel created by Wendy is inspired by the ever-changing landscape along the south coast of England in Sussex. Throughout the seasons and at different times of the day Wendy's landscapes represent moments in time. The undulations of the South Downs and trees in the surrounding countryside contrast with the chalk cliffs and the sea, all offering a wealth of design opportunities.

Wendy has a life-long love of textiles and combines layering fabrics, paint and stitch in her work. Her fabrics are always painted or printed: she uses Sericol screen printing inks; the colour usually being applied after the fabric has been manipulated and stitched.

For this vessel, Pelmet Vilene has been used for the base structure. Carefully selected textured fabrics have then been applied and layered according to the design and worked into with both hand and machine stitching. The stitches are functional, in that they hold the fabrics in place, and also decorative as they show line, form and texture. Additional texture is created with the application of nappy liners and three-dimensional fabric medium, which are worked over with a hot-air tool. Colour is then applied with a palette knife and sponge, using Sericol screen printing ink. Coloured threads are stitched into the design, adding further embellishment and detail. To complete the vessel, machine-wrapped cords are used to represent tree roots and to lace the sides together. The resulting landscape changes as each side is viewed and represents an atmospheric moment in time.

Right: 'Changing Landscape' by Wendy Dolan. This vessel is layered with hand-dyed cotton fabrics and decorated with free-machine embroidery and hand stitch to depict a local scene. It is 244cm (8ft) tall.

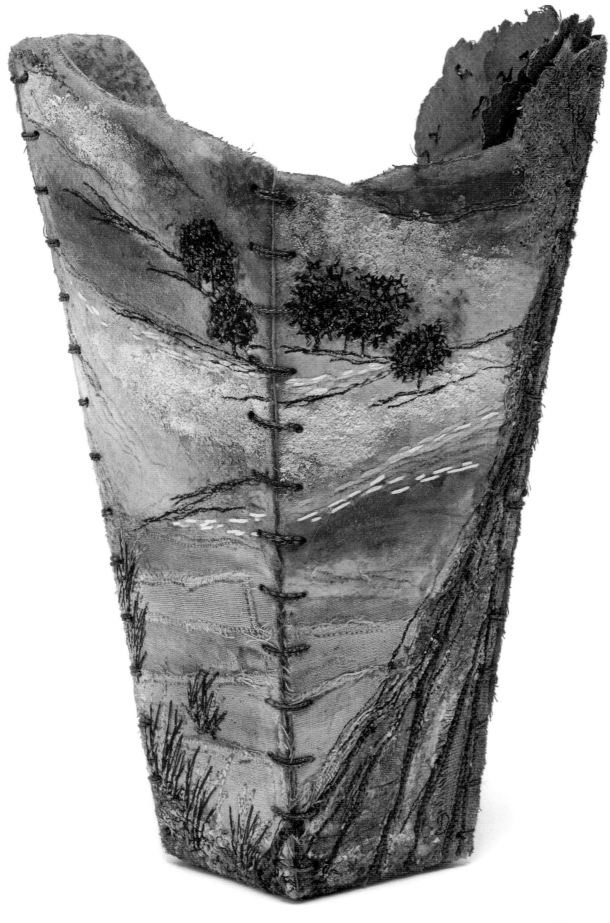

'Brighton Belle' — Mary Drew

'Bonkers boxes' are born of Mary Drew's inherited addiction of 'wombling' – at least that is what her dad called it when he came home from walking the dogs with half a bicycle and an armful of old wood, much to her mother's dismay. He was a hoarder and Mary, too, has this trait, except that her finds are treasure!

Mary likes to collect rejected textile 'stuff', nicely shaped stones and shells and make them into little characters. She likes to see how using this inanimate junk makes naughty, haughty, shy or flamboyant little creatures materialize. She says: 'I hope that what I make has a feel of nostalgia, like thinking back about some strange old aunt who made her own clothes and kept cats – er ... no, sorry, I've just described myself! I hope that they are nostalgic with a twist, something that you cannot quite put your finger on.'

The bodies of Mary's strange little creatures are made from old socks or fine woollen jumpers and are then dressed in scraps of worn and often damaged and unloved vintage fabrics. The eyes and mouths are hand stitched. The creatures are then placed in their new home, which could be a violin case, an old wooden sewing-machine cover or a cigar box – whatever Mary has discovered and stored in her studio. Each little character has a different personality. You will either find them macabre or endearing.

Right: 'Brighton Belle' by Mary Drew. A salvaged box lined with an old map of Brighton, East Sussex, makes a home for a cheeky little dancing creature.

'Physalis' flower spray – Claire Muir

'Each flower is an embellished structure abstracted from organic form. This is how
I used to describe my work when I was at art college and the same still applies today.'

Claire Muir exhibits, lectures and delivers workshops nationally. She has had several articles
published and is sponsored by Madeira Threads. Her early training includes a degree in Art
and Related Arts and the Diploma of Post Graduate Studies, Glasgow School of Art. In 1991
Claire won the Worshipful Company of Drapers Textile Award. Claire designs and makes
flowers, fascinators, tiaras, jewellery and anything else that can be embroidered.

Claire is a free-machine embroiderer who specializes in sewing on cold-water soluble
(CWS) fabric using Madeira Classic 40 (a viscose machine-embroidery thread).

Claire chooses flowers with an open appearance such as lilies, hibiscus, clematis and open
roses, as carnations and tight roses do not suit this embroidered lace technique. Claire is
always inspired by the real flower and often places petals and leaves directly on the CWS
fabric and stitches around them. Sketches also record flower details. Hand-dyed silk or
organza gives the petals a luxurious appearance and small pieces are couched down on
the CWS fabric with the viscose thread before the petals are washed.

Below: A detail of Claire Muir's
'Physalis' flower spray. The full
piece can be seen on the next page.

Wire is an integral part of each flower and is either stitched down the centre or around the edge of each petal. The centres of the flowers are created to echo the original flower, taking care to produce something that has an appearance of light and movement.

Any finished arrangement is never rigid as Claire likes her work to be tweaked and played with. Scale and proportion are important too: Claire's customers need to wear their fascinators, the fascinators must not wear them!

Above: 'Physalis' flower spray by Claire Muir. This beautiful shoulder decoration is 61cm (24in) long and is quite striking when worn on a plain gown. This takes the corsage to a different scale.

On her 'Physalis' flower spray all the flowers have been sewn on CWS and have wires stitched onto the petals before they are washed. Small pieces of fabric have been couched down as she sewed. The petals are embellished with crystals, sequins and beads, while the flower centres are fabric-covered balls with feather or beaded-wire stamens. The turquoise embroidered curls are on wire and the embroidered feathers have been sewn on organza and cut out with a soldering iron. Everything is attached to wire, allowing the spray to be bent into various positions.

'Old Walls' — Judy Williams

This hanging was inspired by a visit to the Cretan island of Spinalonga. Judy Williams was struck by the beauty of the sunlight hitting and bouncing off the old crumbling walls. She had been given a brief to make a three-dimensional piece and the idea of making felt into an old wall using the washing-machine technique appealed to her. Judy has also been inspired by old Cornish walls full of lichen. The two ideas of encrusted crumbling texture came together for this piece.

The bricks of felt were made using a golden to green colour theme with laid pieces of threads and scrim on the surface. This was then roughly stitched into calico and washed at 40 degrees. This gave lovely bumpy and uneven surfaces, which when eventually dried were stitched and embellished with more textured threads. Judy enjoyed the fact that this type of felting can be quite unpredictable. 'Old Walls' has a window of hope in the top and is meant to be seen from both sides. Each brick is different and each side of the brick is different, and these were then stitched together in a haphazard way to make a unified whole. The piece is hung from an old branch from a tree in Judy's garden.

Right: 'Old Walls' by Judy Williams.
Bricks of felt were made in the
washing machine to create very
thick, textured surfaces.
Photographed by Graeme
Brimecombe.

A selection of work – Mary Dean

Mary Dean is an instinctive felt maker; it is remarkable what she can create with a few colours of wool tops, soap and a few hours of her time. She is best known for her accessories: lovely scarves combining wool, muslin and silk, and bags incorporating vintage fabrics and diamanté. One of her latest projects has been making dolls and each doll is different, with jewellery, a hat, a bag and a flower. Mary changes her designs continually; no two pieces are ever the same. Her flowers have wonderful shapes and textures that would grace any coat, hat or knitwear. All her work is made by hand rolling with the occasional use of needle felting for embellishment.

The flowers shown below are made by rubbing and rolling pre-dyed merino tops by hand. The chrysanthemum was made by rolling many small strands of merino tops to create individual petals that were then hand sewn onto a felt base to hold them in place. The daisy was made by rubbing a long rectangle of felt. Before the felt was completely matted, the edges were cut and rubbed to create the effect of separate petals. The rectangle was then rolled to make the flower head. Stranded embroidery yarn was used to make the stamens and the whole thing was then sewn onto a stem. The rose was made in basically the same way as the daisy. Make a long rectangle of felt and roll to create your rose. Stitch onto a small piece of felt to secure the base.

Right: Mary Dean's charming dolls sport jewellery, hats, bags and flowers, all made from felt.

Left: Flowers by Mary Dean, showing, from left to right, chrysanthemum, daisy and rose.

'Small Strata' and 'Soft Remembered Hills'

— Kim Thittichai

'Small Strata' is one of three vessels that were created by me for Hove Museum to be displayed in Preston Manor as part of the Brighton Festival in May 2008. Seven artists were chosen to exhibit their work, which ranged from silver jewellery and ceramics to textiles and steel sculpture. The vessel is 1.2m (4ft) tall and has been created from Pelmet Vilene painted with an acrylic wash for the background colour. Painted Bondaweb has then been applied in various layers and several shades of gold. Artichoke seeds, embossing powders and three-dimension medium were then applied to add texture.

'Soft Remembered Hills' is a vessel that has been formed from heavyweight Lutradur that has been painted with various tones of dilute Procion dye powder and water. You would not normally dye a synthetic fabric with Procion dyes as it would just wash out, however this vessel will not be coming into contact with water so in this case it is perfectly safe. Once the dye had dried the Lutradur was zapped with a 350-watt heat gun and ripped apart to create a lacy, irregular edge. The bronze and silver section of the vessel is created from Bondaweb that has been painted with a thin layer of metallic paints. The machine stitch on this piece is purely functional to hold all the sections together. The rim of the vessel has been cut away with an 18-watt soldering iron.

Opposite left: 'Small Strata' by Kim Thittichai. Painted Bondaweb applied to Pelmet Vilene, decorated with embossing powders, seeds and three-dimensional medium.

Opposite right: 'Soft Remembered Hills' by Kim Thittichai. Layers of Procion-dyed CS 800 (similar to Lutradur 130) distressed with a 350-watt heat gun to create a lacy edge. A section of metallic painted Bondaweb has been added to create a contrast to the matt Lutradur.

Left: Detail of 'Soft Remembered Hills' showing the painted Bondaweb section.

Scale

Working on a larger scale can change the way you need to think about your work. Will it stand up by itself? Does it need to be supported? Will it be viewed from all sides? The work also needs to be secure – you don't want it to fall on anyone. Your final question and probably most important is 'How will you move your work?' There are many things to consider, but don't be put off. A well-planned installation or single piece of work of a larger scale can make an exhibition more interesting to visit. The following four examples of large-scale work illustrate various ways of addressing some of these issues.

Right: 'Sarracenia' by Jayne Routley, which represent, from left to right, hearing, smell, taste, sight and touch. These wonderful pieces range in height from 183 x 200cm (6–6½ft). They are taller than most adults and give you a feeling of awe when you walk among them.

'Sarracenia' – Jayne Routley

These 'plants' were made for an exhibition entitled 'Unveiled' in 2006. Jayne Routley started with the question 'What is unveiled?' and moved from there to explore the question 'How do we reveal things?' People explore the world around them with their senses.

Sight   *Hearing*   *Taste*   *Touch*   *Smell*

Jayne says: 'Each one is important for us to understand and discover our environment; we use them to experience everything. While thinking about "unveiled" on a trip to the Hampton Court Flower Show I saw some carnivorous plants. I was amazed by the shapes and forms, the colours and the variety. They entrap their prey by using their senses against them. I imagined what it would be like if these plants were 2m (6½ft) tall!'

This body of work has been exhibited in various venues and it is always fascinating to see the response of the public when they realize the pieces can be interacted with. 'Sight' has areas of highly decorative and textured stitch and fairy lights. 'Hearing' has a set of headphones that can be taken out and listened to playing music by Fields of the Nephilim.'Taste' has pockets in which Jayne has put peanuts for salt, boiled sweets for sweet. 'Touch' is more highly textured and is placed on a vibrating plate so the whole piece quivers to the touch. 'Smell' has various sachets of herbs and air fresheners that scent the air around this piece.

Jayne continues: 'Constructed with hand-painted felt and machine stitched with a variety of fabrics, each one represents one of our senses. They are interactive: one contains things to test your taste buds, another has headphones to listen to my favourite music, one vibrates, one has patches with different smells, and one has pretty lights and things to observe!'

Making work that is three dimensional and that will stand up by itself has many challenges. Do you make a frame and cover it? Do you want your piece to stand up by itself? Once you get over 60cm (2ft) in height most products will bend unless supported. Jayne chose to use Formafelt. This is a product that can be soaked in hot water and moulded around a chicken-wire frame. Once the frame was removed the Formafelt created a strong enough structure to support itself. Each 'plant' is embellished with hand and machine embroidery and is painted with a combination of acrylic paint and Procion dye.

'Hive' and 'Marisha's Forest' – Nikki Parmenter

Nikki Parmenter trained initially as a fine artist at Manchester Polytechnic, gaining a
1st class honours degree and an MA. She has exhibited widely since the mid-1990s and her
work has become increasingly more complicated. She has gone from two-dimensional images
on paper to sculptural textiles.

Nikki bought a sewing machine two-and-a-half years ago and has not looked back since.
She is entirely self-taught and relies on textile books that demonstrate specific techniques
such as bonding fabrics, incorporating metal into work and so on. From this she has gradually
developed her own techniques and feels that her work is unique as she always includes
some type of narrative element; the pieces exist for a reason. Nikki is particularly
inspired by mythology and symbolism.

The two featured pieces here contain a huge range of materials: beads, hosepipe, pipe
cleaners, wool, Funky Foam, acetate, felt, fabrics, plastic gems, jewellery, hair decorations,
Christmas ornaments, acrylic paint, wood, gel pens, a kitchen sink drainer sprayed gold, the
underside of carpet underlay, metals, car spray paint, Angelina fibre, wire, plastics and much
more. Nikki collects objects that are interesting and incorporates them into pieces of work. A
trip to her local hardware shop usually provides some kind of useful material to use.

The two pieces shown here are called 'Hive' and 'Marish's Forest' and are 1.5m (5ft) and 2m
(7ft) tall respectively. They are formed around plant obelisks purchased from a local garden
centre. Nikki had to lengthen the legs of the obelisks to get the height she needed.

'Hive' was inspired by the fact that over the summer it was reported in the press that
bee numbers were declining and this led Nikki to investigate the history, symbolism and
mythology surrounding bees and honey. The piece features an Aztec bee god, Egyptian bee
keepers, Cupid, a bee-eater bird, a medieval beehive, the Indian bee goddess, and various
different types of bees and honeycombs. The title is meant to convey a 'hive' of activity.
Warm golds, yellows and oranges with blue have been used to create a contrast.

'Marisha's Forest' was inspired by a line from an Indian mythology book. Marisha was the
goddess of the night-time forest. Marisha herself is near the top of the column and opposite
her on the other side is the moon god Chandra. Surrounding them are birds, animals and
fish that are found in India. There are fish at the base and then other creatures are added in
a spiral form – a frog, fish, tiger, crocodile, flamingo, tiger, parrot – so the column starts in the
water and ends in the sky. Nikki wanted this piece to be a mysterious purple and green colour
to create the impression of night-time.

Above: Detail of 'Hive' by Nikki
Parmenter.

Opposite: 'Marisha's Forest' (right),
by Nikki Parmenter, is 2m (7ft) tall,
while 'Hive' (far right), also by Nikki,
is 1.5m (5ft) tall. These remarkable
pieces are so ornate you cannot at
first appreciate the amount of work
involved.

'Women Through Their Ages' — Susan Chapman

Susan Chapman says: 'My main inspiration comes from people, the way they live, the way they interact with each other and how they deal with the trials and tribulations that they are faced with throughout their lives.'

Colour is of paramount importance to Susan and she is very much influenced by Matisse's use of bright colour and simple repeating images. Emotionally the artists that also influence her are Eva Hesse, Louise Bourgeois, Andy Goldsworthy, Anthony Gormley, Anthony Frost, Jim Dine, Sue Dove and Dorothy Caldwell; an eclectic mix but a constant source of excitement.

Although Susan's roots are in quilt-making, she now collages her dyed, painted, printed, discharged and screen-printed fabrics, then stitches and embellishes her pieces by hand and machine. She works in two and three dimensions and is particularly interested in book forms as well as large-scale work.

Susan is now working on a new body of work taken from life drawing in a local park, watching the relationship of people, one to another. This activity demands very fast sketches as people walk towards her, chatting and enjoying their companionship. She is very excited by this new and more abstract method of working.

Right: 'Out of the Mouths of Babes' from Women Through Their Ages by Susan Chapman is 137cm (4½ft) tall. This piece represents the infant stage in a woman's life.

Far right: 'I Want to Break Free' by the second of Susan's pieces, is 175cm (5¾ft) tall and represents the teenager, studded, pierced and laced in denim and leather.

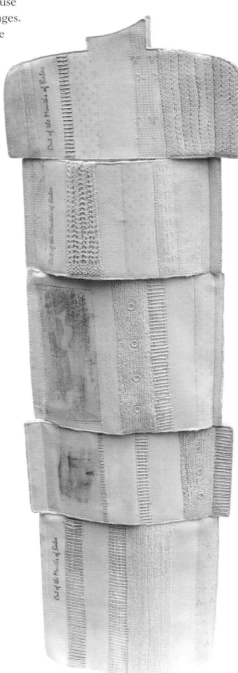

This installation, 'Women Through Their Ages', deals with the issues of age, each piece representing a different time in a woman's life. It consists of four sculptures, each one having a sentence associated with it. It is this text that has inspired each piece. Some time has been spent considering how the various ages could be represented in surface textile textures and then the appropriate fabrics have been used as described below.

The first piece represents the child; it is worked in mainly white and silver, using white knitting, delicate pink and blue stripes and checks, and terry towelling nappies. The phrase associated with this piece is 'Out of the Mouths of Babes'.

The second represents the teenager; it is worked mainly in denim and black leather, embellished with some lacing, rhinestones and banana bars. The phrase associated with this piece is from a song by the band Queen: 'I Want to Break Free'.

The third represents the prime of life; this is worked mainly in green and uses flowers to represent the blooming and bountiful nature of pregnancy. The phrase associated with this piece is 'In the Prime of Life'.

Finally the old lady is represented; she is worked in red and purple, with knitting, muslin and felt used for the textural surfaces. This piece is inspired by Jenny Joseph's poem *Warning* with this line: 'When I am an Old Woman I Shall Wear Purple'.

Below left: 'In the Prime of Life' by Susan Chapman is 175cm (5¾ft) tall.

Below right: 'When I Am an Old Woman I Shall Wear Purple' by Susan Chapman is 152cm (5ft) tall.

Tassels – Sue Davies

These tassels were Sue Davies's first-year project. Very basic tassel making was one of the techniques included in the first year. Sue took a couple of metres of old hemp rope that had been donated from the local theatre and started to deconstruct it. The whole process made a terrible mess but it was worth it – these two tassels were what resulted from Sue's hard work. The 'Medusa' tassel (far right) is 1.5m (5ft) long and the deconstructed rope has been plaited for the 'skirt' and plaited and wired to create the 'ruff'. There are sections of hand-made felt, and wooden beads were added for decoration.

The rag-rugged tassel (right) is almost 2m (7ft) long. The 'skirt' of the tassel is deconstructed hemp rope with fine nylon filament and glass beads added. The 'ruff' is created from a panel of natural fabrics hooked and stitched through rug canvas.

Right: Tassel by Sue Davies. This piece, made from deconstructed hemp rope with a rag-rugged 'skirt', is 2m (7ft) long.

Left: 'Medusa' tassel by Sue Davies. Made from deconstructed, plaited and wired hemp rope, this tassel is 1.5m (5ft) long.

Inspiration – Where to Find It

This chapter shows where eight artists find their inspiration. I have chosen these particular artists to demonstrate eight types of inspiration: colour, material, people, process, words, drawing, music and place. We are all inspired by different things at different times. It can depend on your mood, emotional state, two shapes next to each other or simply which way the wind is blowing. What you were once excited by several years ago will change as you develop and learn new and different ways of looking at and interpreting the world around you. New experiences such as travelling to an exotic destination or an exhibition can be the starting point for a whole new train of thought. How work is exhibited can also change the way you experience it. Being able to interact with an artist's work adds an exciting dimension. It is important to get out and about if you can. Look at different types of art, not just textiles.

Right: Part of 'Connected With Colour' by Ruth Issett, exhibited at the Knit and Stitch show in London and Birmingham in 2008. The pieces demonstrate print, stitch and appliqué.

Colour – Ruth Issett

Ruth Issett is well known as a wonderful tutor and the author of four seminal books on the subjects of printing, dyeing, paper colouring and use of different media. Her main inspiration is colour. Having taught City & Guilds courses for many years, Ruth turned freelance in 2001, which meant she could travel more and reach students further afield. She is able to help any student to be more confident and positive when working with dyes and colour. Her teaching is centred on understanding the materials that students wish to work with and if possible how they can most suitably use them in their own work. Whether it is colour mixing, dyeing or printing on fabric and paper, the way you work after being taught by Ruth will change forever. Having attended workshops with Ruth myself I now dye all my own threads and fabric with no fear whatsoever.

Ruth recently created an inspirational travelling exhibition entitled 'Connected with Colour', which was striking for the sheer scale and simple beauty of the work. Lengths of cotton organdie had been initially dye painted to create a glorious bright and subtle palette. Some sections were then printed and other areas overlaid with additional layers of carefully selected colour fabric as well as hand stitch and simple machine couching of brilliant contrasting threads. Ruth gradually built the whole exhibition, section by section, not to a large master plan, but by creating one piece, then adding another, then creating another until she felt that whole show began to interpret her original design idea. This meant that the exhibition could be displayed differently at each venue, in order to adjust it to the particular venue, its aspect and location. The layers of colour and texture invited you into a carefully considered space where you were allowed to interact and actually touch the work. It was like wandering through a rainbow.

Ruth says: 'The responses were incredible; one lady wanted to cry, another became very excitable, but most of all I was thrilled that youngsters were keen to walk through it, to engage with it by having their photos taken with it!'

Material – Clyde Olliver

I first saw Clyde Olliver's work 'Construction' at the Barbican in London in 1996 as part of the remarkable exhibition 'Revelation', curated by Lesley Millar. The sheer scale and uncomplicated magnificence of the piece astounded me. I had never seen anything like it before. Constructed from wool, felt and slate in natural shades of grey and brown, it stretched above me like a beautiful monolith. The next body of work I saw was 'The Big Stitch'. This travelling one-man exhibition was of smaller, more intimate pieces.

Stones and slate had been drilled, carved and stitched to create very pleasing and simple, but nevertheless decorative surfaces. Much of Clyde's work falls between sculpture and embroidery, since it consists of stitched slate or other suitable stone. Sometimes the work is primarily sculptural – with stitch used as a means of mark making or as an aid to construction. At other times the work is primarily embroidery – with stitch the main element of the work.

Clyde Olliver started stitching and making objects in paper and cardboard at around the age of six and has worked through a variety of jobs including working as studio assistant to tapestry maker Marta Rogoyska in the 1980s. When Clyde was searching for direction at a crucial time in his career he was inspired by the materials his father used as a builder, which included roofing slate. Experimenting with these materials has helped to define how and with which materials he now works. Clyde lives in the English Lake District, where the rocky landscape provides both materials and inspiration.

Clyde's more recent work 'Aggregate' is an ongoing project of large-scale embroideries based on the human figure, constructed from small, stitched tesserae of slate, which has come out of his year as Embroiderers' Guild scholar.

Right: 'Construction' by Clyde Olliver, shown at the Barbican, London, in 1996. The piece is 244 x 152cm (8ft x 5ft). Photographed by Damian Chapman.

Below left: 'Westmorland Knot' by Clyde Olliver, made from drilled and stitched slate and measures 15.5 x 24cm (6 x 9½in).

Below right: 'Study' by Clyde Olliver, made from scratched slate with surface pigmentation, drilled and stitched and measures 19 x 15cm (7½ x 6in)

People – Judy Martin

Judy Martin is a painter and teacher and is also known as the author of many practical art books. She studied painting and printmaking at Maidstone College of Art and went on to complete a two-year postgraduate course at Reading University. Judy was a freelance writer and editor for 15 years and has subsequently worked in adult education and at a mental health centre facilitating groups in art, craft and ceramics.

Left: Detail from 'Entertaining the Dog' showing lacy tights, tissue and paint. See pages 108–109 for the full image.

Her work runs in series, sometimes exploring the potential of a single image from a newspaper or magazine. This could range across a broad subject such as movement or dance or the form of the local landscape. In recent years her work has primarily been concerned with figure and portrait subjects drawn from a variety of sources. A current series is based on old family photographs from the early part of the 20th century. The images are allowed to evolve in ways that may take them beyond the original subject, resulting in a combination of observed and invented elements. Surface qualities are important; each picture is uniquely formed by the material and processes used. I find her use of fabric, such as old tights, pillowcases and paint crosses boundaries we aren't supposed to cross!

Judy started using fabric in her paintings simply as a pattern element. She collects remnants, scraps and fabrics from second-hand outlets. They are chosen for the visual qualities of colour and pattern, and for being of a suitable weight for applying to paper or canvas. Judy also likes the texture of the fabric contrasting with the liquid movement of the paint and the plasticity of its dried textures, so there is more variety in the surface effects.

'Entertaining the Dog' is based on an old family photograph, which suggests the idea of old-fashioned patterned and faded fabrics. Because the foreground figure on the right is dominant (see overleaf), Judy wanted a pattern with strong qualities, but not so loud as to overwhelm the remainder of the image. The dress is cut from an old pillowcase, which had just the right qualities. Initially Judy intended to paint more over the pattern, but if the shape is just right it creates form, often without further intervention. The standing figure on the left has a more dynamic pattern, which is held by the self-contained shape. Judy has added paint to this to indicate a quality of light that was in the photo.

The smaller background figures needed to be in some way fainter than the others, but not without detail. For these, Judy used pieces of lace in muted colours, adding paint to integrate them with the yellow background. This area was harder to get right, and it was reworked quite heavily. In some sections Judy had to take off the fabric and glue on a new piece, then repaint. The lace is also more difficult to apply because the gauzy texture does not hold the adhesive as well as a woven cotton fabric. Judy uses PVA adhesive to apply both fabric and paper collage.

Left: 'Entertaining The Dog' by Judy Martin. Judy cleverly combines fabric and paper collage with paint, sometimes overpainting the fabric to tone it down or to add detailing or tones.

Process – Myriam Tripet

I met Myriam Tripet when she was a student on one of my summer schools. She had flown over from Sweden where she lives. I was struck by the way she used her materials. Myriam showed no fear in throwing colour or materials together to create beautiful samples. She works in a very intuitive way, not quite knowing what the finished piece will be until it is completed, literally designing through process.

Below: 'Memoir du Temps' by Myriam Tripet. Black felt is decorated with painted Bondaweb and dyed scrim to create soft shadows and lines.

Myriam has an innate sense of colour and form and a talent for heavily machined embroidery. She has worked with many artists and textile tutors, testing and researching new techniques while developing a style of her own.

In 1995, a meeting with Ina Georgeta Statescu, a Romanian artist, marked a turning point in her creative process. Fibres such as wool, silk and flax are used to build up surfaces, which are then stitched with toning yarns and enhanced with metallic. Nature in all its colourful majesty is her main inspiration.

Below: 'Promenade d'Automne' by Myriam Tripet. Various hand-dyed threads and fabrics have been heavily machine embroidered into cold-water soluble fabric to create a highly textured and colourful piece.

Words – Angie Hughes

Angie Hughes is a textile artist and tutor based in Ledbury, Herefordshire. She has been interested in textiles since she left school, although only discovered creative embroidery in 1994 when she began studying City & Guilds at Malvern Hills College. While a student she won the prestigious Charles Henry Foyle Trust Award for Stitched Textiles with her piece 'Unfolding Word' and had 'Shroud' accepted for Art of the Stitch. She carried on her studies at Gloucestershire College with Liz Harding after which she discovered a talent for teaching and currently teaches in her studio, Ledbury Artplace and for guilds and groups all over the country.

Her artwork is inspired by many themes but especially poetry or text and the natural world, particularly plant forms. 'Wake Up (The Ledbury Rap)' was inspired by a poem written by Mark Stevenson. It is about the town of Ledbury and all the characters therein. The piece is wall hung and is created from recycled and odd strips of fabric including calico, scrim and various interlinings.

Right: 'Wake Up (The Ledbury Rap)' by Angie Hughes was inspired by a poem by Mark Stevenson.

Below: Detail of 'Wake Up' showing the heavily textured, printed and stitch-applied words.

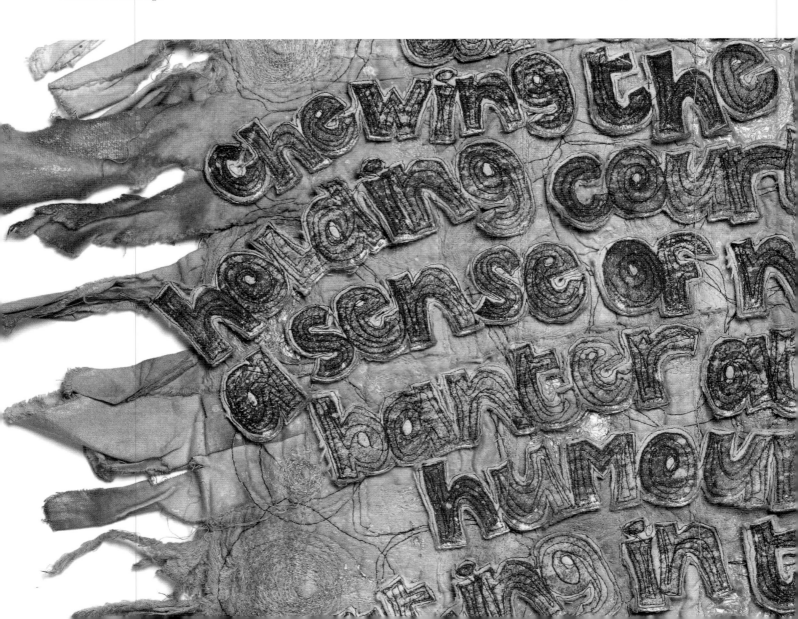

wake up you've got
see what you've got
a house on stilts
a crazy town clock
a welsh town crier
a few billy liars
& launderette
with white driers
you've got the white hart
heaven & the town clerk
broken glass
bottles in the park
a fine street sweeper
with time to talk
a market a theatre
places to walk
places to eat places to stay
in dog kill wood
theyre making hay
hip hop pickers in the season
bring a little colour
rhyme and reason
saturday night lads on a bender
simple as that no hidden agenda
gender benders money lenders
sad eyed lonely mail senders
masquerading
pavement parading
going on the weather
did i say its raining
silver hill staggers with perfection
he knows his nose knows the election
tony harry whispering smith green
chewing the fat then taking a piss
talking carp in the prince of wales
a sense of nonsense here in the tails
humour within rumour
sitting in the softest bar
should have got in sooner
heres to the fool in all his glory
heres to the town
and end of story

Drawing – Lee Brown

Lee Brown originally trained as a commercial artist at Hornsea School of Art. She worked for many years as a commercial artist in her own studio. Later on she attended the London College of Fashion and took a degree in Embroidered Textiles as a mature student. With a family to consider and the slow demise of commercial art due to the upcoming wonders of computer-generated graphic design, Lee retrained as an adult-education tutor and began teaching City & Guilds Embroidery and Patchwork and Quilting. Many hundreds of students have been taught by Lee over the past 14 years, several winning national prizes and many going on to higher education.

It is Lee's strength as a draftsperson that really sets her work apart from others in the field. There are many remarkable quilters, but Lee's work is renowned for its depth of field and perspective. She is well known for her many interpretations of Gothic-style ceilings and buildings. 'Silent Echoes' has been worked from a drawing of a derelict crypt Lee made when she was touring Belgium on holiday. The quilt is constructed from hand-dyed and painted natural fabrics using Procion and Helazerin dye. Favoured fabrics tend to be calico and other firm cottons. Viscose satin is used for its wonderful light-reflecting qualities. The quilt is around 1.8 × 1.2m (6 × 4ft) and is wall hung; you really feel that you could walk into it.

Opposite: 'Silent Echoes' by Lee Brown, hand dyed and individually pieced by hand with chiffon overlays to create shadows.

Below: Detail of 'Silent Echoes'.

Music – Bobby Britnell

Bobby Britnell is passionate about everything she does, whether it is teaching, creating her marvellous work, looking after her family or Morris dancing! Bobby is a musician for a local Morris dance group as well as being a dancer in the team. It is therefore not surprising that one of her inspirations is music and dance, as it offers many starting points for exploring pattern, colour and movement.

'The Morning Star' is a quilt that reflects a free interpretation of a Morris dance. The tune played for this dance is a traditional tune and is also called 'The Morning Star' and in the quilt the written notes form an integral part of the piece of work. The fabric used is natural scoured cotton, which has been home dyed using Procion dyes and pieced to form a whole cloth. Shapes are applied using Bondaweb and held in place with machine quilting. Some areas are coloured with Markal Paintstiks and printing provides additional emphasis. The work is finished with machine quilting and a bound edge. The piece portrays the vibrancy of the dancing and reflects an energy and vitality present in the Border Morris style of dancing.

Left: Detail of 'The Morning Star' by Bobby Britnell showing the different shapes of machine stitch that hold the piece together.

Above: 'Morning Star' by Bobby Britnell.

Bobby continues to explore and develop her own individual style of working, with the entire process of designing and drawing being of equal importance. She enjoys changing the surface of fabrics through dyeing, colouring, printing and stitching, with the drawn marks becoming increasingly more important in her current work.

Bobby's background is in theatre where she made elaborate costumes for the *Black and White Minstrel Show, Talk of the Town* and many West End musicals. She later learnt the skills of tailoring, before training as a teacher.

Place – Gwen Hedley

Gwen Hedley started her working life as a primary-school teacher, with creative arts as her specialism. Drawing and making have always featured largely in her life and, many years on, she began using stitch as an expressive art form, beginning her associations with embroidery.

Gwen is an inspirational tutor and the author of *Surfaces for Stitch* (see Further Reading, page 126). She is drawn to worn surfaces, where line, image and colour have disintegrated with the passing of time. Sources include torn images from stripped hoardings and the surface qualities of museum artefacts. Her recent work is concerned with the power of the sea, and how its movements process the surfaces of stone, wood, metal and other flotsam and jetsam. Crevices are packed with shingle. Papers, plastics and cloth scraps are folded and half buried. Whatever humankind leaves upon the shore, the sea consumes it, and returns it in gentler form – brash colours faded and dulled, hard edges softened and surfaces smoothed.

'Red, White and Black' and 'Earth Source' are two pieces from her 'Relic' series. This body of work evolved through her study of the Dungeness shoreline in Kent, from where she has collected all manner of flotsam and jetsam, in an ever-widening range of media.

She says: 'I called the series "Relics", because the definitions seemed appropriate for what I wanted to convey. I always feel that the found objects and fragments that I collect are somehow imbued with the sense of peace and beauty that I find on Dungeness.

> *Relic; definitions:*
> *An object kept for its association with the past: a memento.*
> *Something cherished for its antiquity and beauty.*
> *An antiquity that has survived the passage of time.*

'The relics are my response to the tying, binding and wrapping that is evident on the shore, where objects are grouped and often secured in bundles, on sand shelves, on the pebbles or collected and then left abandoned in sheds. I was also taken with the idea of both organizing and assembling the discarded, while creating items that were decorative, and at the same time symbolic of the environment in which they were found.'

Left: Detail of 'Earth Source' showing wrapped finds from the beach.

Right: 'Earth Source' by Gwen Hedley, part of her Relic series. This piece is 61cm (24in) long.

Below: 'Red, White and Black' by Gwen Hedley. This piece is 25.5cm (10in) long.

Where Next?

Working in groups

It is hard to be creative and keep generating new work when you work on your own. Working in groups is a great opportunity to share ideas and benefit from group evaluation. But there needs to be a reason to get together and stay together.

Teaching around the country as I do, I meet many diverse groups, from embroiderers' and quilters' guilds to the smallest group of friends that get together once a year. In my experience there seem to be three basic types of group.

1 Guilds

Embroiderers' and quilters' guilds have a constitution and an elected committee. Some guilds have spin-off groups that organize their own workshops and lectures separately as well as the main guild. Guilds have open membership where anyone can become a member. An annual fee is paid and then a small fee on the door every time you attend a meeting. Guilds meet the same day every month and meetings usually last two-and–a-half to three hours. Having been a speaker at many guild meetings I am often aware that a small amount of members appear to do all the work and are very often short of volunteers for help. Do be prepared to do your share.

There should be a guild in your area – see page 126 for further information.

2 Post education

A good time to start a group is when you finish a course in education. Your group is already established, you know you want to carry on with your work and develop your own style and maybe exhibit once in a while. Where and how often will you meet? How many do you need to make a successful group? There are many groups that meet regularly and all the members take it in turns to help run the group. There are several calls on members' time, from finance to booking rooms, booking tutors and keeping up the membership. You all need to agree on many issues. The most important thing is that you all need to work together and respect and value the other members. There are always a few who hang back and do not volunteer to help; try not to be one of those.

A well-organized group will have a healthy membership with perhaps a waiting list. Most groups will book regular workshops with tutors to help keep their skills honed. Some groups just meet together to discuss their work. You have to decide what is best for you.

It may be that not every class that finishes a course will be suitable to run as a post-education group but it is always worth trying.

Left: Close-up detail of 'Marisha's Forest' by Nikki Parmenter. For the full piece, see page 97.

3 Professional exhibiting groups

Other groups are created as exhibiting groups that support an artist's professional development such as the Practical Study Group and the 62 Group (see page 126 for contact details). These groups are usually made up from professional tutors and textile artists and entry will be decided by a jury of members. Some groups like to interview you personally with a portfolio; others will ask for a CV or personal statement and pictures of your work via email or CD.

Exhibitions usually tour nationally and occasionally internationally.

Starting your own group

One of the most well-organized groups I have worked with is The Textile Workshop. They are a post City & Guilds Study Group and have kindly given permission to include their 'aims of the group' for your benefit.

The Textile Workshop
The Aims of the group are as follows;

- *To provide a self-help situation in a friendly and relaxed atmosphere.*
- *To encourage individual expression and development in a non-competitive environment.*
- *To improve the status of our craft in general and promote high standards of design and workmanship.*
- *To present work as a group for exhibition.*

At the meeting held at Wickham on 24th February 1994, which was attended by 11 members, the following guidelines were drawn up.

1. *The group will meet each month on the third Thursday except in August and December.*
2. *For practical reasons the group should not exceed 25 members.*
3. *A member, who does not attend at least five monthly meetings during the year without good reason shall, after a reminder, have their membership terminated at the end of the year (September). If they wish at any time to rejoin, they may do so on payment of the subscription, unless there is a waiting list, in which case their name shall be placed on it.*
4. *The annual membership fee will be 20 pounds per year plus 12 pounds for each meeting with an outside tutor, or five pounds for a meeting taken by one of our members. This fee will be waived for that day for the member who takes the workshop.*
5. *Associate Members will be required to pay five pounds per year to receive information each month, but will not be eligible to attend meetings of exhibit. If an Associate Member wishes to apply for full membership, they will be given priority.*

These guidelines and the aims of the Group do not form a formal constitution and therefore the Group has no elected committee nor is led by one person. The responsibilities for organising meetings, tutors, bookings, refreshments and the treasurer's post are divided up between members, and will change each September. This set of guidelines will be reviewed each July.

These are the kinds of guidelines that need to be drawn up and discussed with any potential group.

How do you find a group when you are on your own? The internet is good place to start: put a few key words into a search engine and see what you come up with. Try 'textiles' or 'stitch' and the name of your town. There are many blogs online now, which can be a good read and may link you to others also wanting to join or start a group. Your local Embroiderers' Guild is also a good place to start or you could try putting up notices in your local library.

This piece has been written by Hazel Imbert, one of the main instigators of 'Necrotex' whose work is featured on pages 64–65. I invited her write about how her group is developing:

> *Is there life after a textile course? Well, yes. Out of the group which created the 'Necrotex' exhibition grew Angelico, a loosely set up group of ten textile artists (loosely in the sense of being comfortable working together without the need for a constitution, bank account or other formalities). They have created further exhibitions – 'Maternal', 'Rings' and 'Faded Glory'.*
>
> *At the time of writing, two exhibitions are in progress: 'Family Ties' (based on deconstructed ties); and a street art event using Tyvek boiler suits. The group also produces a variety of work for sale at artists' open houses locally, twice a year.*
>
> *The group meets regularly for informal workshops, where skills are shared along with food and talk. Decisions are made about next steps, and everyone is kept informed through the message board of their (very basic) website.*
>
> *A further development has been the formation of Moving Stitchers out of Angelico. Four of the group have recently set up a community arts project aimed at sharing textile skills with all ages and abilities across the community.*
>
> *Still in its early stages, the project is mobile and responsive; able to adapt to the interests and abilities of any group, ranging from 'How to Knit' to the upper reaches of embellishing. So much of textile work is portable and can be done with easy-to-acquire tools and materials; the group operates under the banner 'Working with textiles is cheap, entertaining and relatively harmless, and stimulates creativity.' So far, the response has been good, and workshops have been held with young people with severe physical disabilities, with primary-age children, and with a general group.*
>
> *Current plans include having a presence at local events, doing something visible and inclusive, such as knitting on giant needles and inviting people to have a go, or knitting a community scarf to which people can add a stitch, a row, a bobble or a tassel.*
>
> *There is a basic website to facilitate creating connections as well as providing information. Funding applications will go out when the group has a year's work documented in support.*

Tutoring

Having taught so many students over the years I, like many other tutors, could be said to have trained my own competition. This can sometimes create problems if you are all working on the same 'patch'. I have happily given up running workshops in felt making, rag rugging and silk paper to name but a few and several of my ex-students are now teaching these. I am now left with the more 'difficult' subjects of design and colour but that is my choice. It is always very satisfying to hear on the grapevine that one of your students has just taught a brilliant or thought-provoking workshop.

It is important to remember that your tutor has spent many years developing his or her techniques and processes and it would be very unfair to start teaching what you learnt from them without their permission. Most tutors respect others by not copying what they do.

All professional tutors now need to be members of the IFL (Institute for Learning), the professional body for teachers, trainers, tutors, student teachers and assessors in the further education and skills sector. Tutors are required to complete a minimum of 30 hours' CPD (continuing professional development) every year.

Being a travelling textile tutor has its ups and downs but it is truly the most satisfying and rewarding thing I have ever done. I had a slower start than most as I was the odd one doing strange melty things and no one quite knew what to do with me, but things move on and I am now very busy and almost able to support myself. If you find something you love, pursue it and do not let go. It will be worth it in the end.

So, what is next for you? Are you going sit there and think about it or are you going to get on with it? As we are all regularly reminded, life is short! Go and fetch your needles and thread and stitch something now! Or paint something, or draw something, or knit something. Let me know how you get on.

There is a website with course outlines, worksheets and contact details to help you in your quest to keep working and inspired. www.experimentaltextiles.com

Below: Decorated monoprint by Frances Davis.

Further information

Featured artists

Bobby Britnell
Email: bobby@bobbybritnell.co.uk
Website: www.bobbybritnell.co.uk

Lee Brown
Email: lee@leebrowndesigns.co.uk
Website: www.leebrowndesigns.co.uk

Carol Coleman
Email: carole.coleman@btopenworld.com

Sue Chapman
Email: susan@susanchapman.com

Mary Drew
Email: marymoo@hotmail.com

Wendy Dolan
Email: wendy.dolan@ntlworld.com
Website: www.wendydolan.co.uk

Jill Flower
Email: jill.flower@yahoo.co.uk

Gwen Hedley
Website: www.practicalstudygroup.co.uk

Angie Hughes
Email: angie@angiehughes.com
Website: www.angiehughes.com

Ruth Isset
Email: ruth.issett@btinternet.com

Debbie Lyddon
Email: debbielyddon@hotmail.co.uk

Judy Martin
Email: judymtn@aol.com
Website: www.judymartin.co.uk

Claire Muir
Email: info@clairemuir.co.uk
Website: www.clairemuir.co.uk

Clyde Olliver
Email: clyde.olliver@hotmail.co.uk
Website: www.clydeolliver.com

Nikki Parmenter
Email: info@nikkiparmenter.co.uk
Website: www.nikkiparmenter.co.uk

Jaynie Rawling
Email: jaynierawling@hotmail.co.uk

Jayne Routley
Email: ladylazarus@ntlworld.com
Website: www.ladylazarus.co.uk

Kim Thittichai
Email: info@kimthittichai.com
Website: www.kimthittichai.com

Myriam Tripet
Website: www.art-textile.ch

Judy Williams
Email: judywilliams9@googlemail.com
Website: www.judy-williams.com

Kim's students can be contacted via her email:
info@kimthittichai.com
Gwenda Baker, Liz Carter, Karen Cunningham, Sue Davies, Mary Dean, Eleanor Fielder, Jean Gerrard, Helen Igo, Hazel Imbert, Morna McGibbon, Jane Potter, Amanda Simmonds, Lucy Spearman.
These websites have been created since these students finished college:
Angelico: www.angelico.org.uk
Threads: www.threads.org.uk
Necrotex: www.necrotex.org.uk
Moving Stitchers: www.movingstitchers.org.uk

Further reading

Beal, Margaret, *Fusing Fabric: Creative Cutting, Bonding and Mark Making with the Soldering Iron*, Batsford, 2005

Beaney, Jan, *The Art of the Needle: Designing in Fabric and Thread*, Ebury Press, 1988

Beaney, Jan and Littlejohn, Jean, *A Complete Guide to Creative Embroidery*, Batsford, 1997

Beaney, Jan and Littlejohn, Jean, *Stitch Magic: Ideas and Interpretation*, Batsford, 2005

Caprara, Julia, *Exploring Colour*, d4daisy, 2008

Edmonds, Janet, *Three-dimensional Embroidery*, Batsford, 2005

Issett, Ruth, *Glorious Papers: Techniques for Applying Colour to Paper*, Batsford, 2001

Issett, Ruth, *Colour on Cloth: Create Stunning Effects with Dye on Fabric*, Batsford, 2004

Issett, Ruth, *Print, Pattern and Colour*, Batsford, 2007

Jerstorp, Karin, and Kohlmark, Eva, *The Textile Design Book: Understanding and Creating Patterns Using Texture, Shape and Colour*, A&C Black, 1989

Genders, Carolyn, *Sources of Inspiration: For Ceramics and the Applied Arts*, A&C Black, 2004

Greenlees, Kay, *Creating Sketchbooks for Embroiderers and Textile Artists*, Batsford 2005

Hedley, Gwen, *Surfaces for Stitch: Plastics, Film and Fabric*, Batsford, 2004

Messent, Jan, *Design with Pattern*, Madeira Thread (UK) Ltd, 1998

Neill, William; Murphy, Pat; Ackerman, Diane, *By Natures Design*, Chronicle Books 1993

Rottger, Ernst, *Creative Paper Craft*, Batsford 1961

Textile groups

The Practical Study Group (PSG)
Website: www.practicalstudygroup.co.uk
A diverse group of well-qualified, nationally and internationally renowned textile artists and tutors, who have established a reputation for excellence.

62 Group
Website: www.62group.org.uk
One of the most exciting groups of textile artists in the UK.

Embroiderers' Guild
Apartment 41
Hampton Court Palace
Surrey KT8 9AU
Tel: +44 (0)20 8943 1229
Fax: +44 (0)20 8977 9882
Email: administrator@embroiderersguild.com
Website: www.embroiderersguild.com
The Embroiderers Guild can direct you to regional guilds in your area.

The Quilters' Guild of The British Isles
St Anthony's Hall
York, YO1 7PW
Tel: +44 (0)1904 613242
Fax: +44 (0)1904 632394
Email: info@quiltersguild.org.uk
Website: www.quiltersguild.org.uk
The Quilters Guilds can direct you to regional guilds in your area.

Right: The 'Necrotex' girls, who worked on the project shown on page 64.

Workshops

This list is by no means complete – there are many independent venues offering excellent workshops across the UK. All the venues listed run a variety of excellent workshops – see the websites for details.

Bobby Britnell
Moor Hall Farmhouse,
Bettws-y-Crwyn,
Newcastle on Clun,
Shropshire SY7 8PH
Email: bobby@bobbybritnell.co.uk
Website: www.bobbybritnell.co.uk
Bobby also teaches with Ruth Issett (ruth.issett@btinternet.com) and together they run a series of workshops entitled Working Together near Craven Arms in Shropshire.

Art Van Go
The Studios
1 Stevenage Road
Knebworth
Hertfordshire SG3 6AN
Tel: +44 (0)1438 814946
fax: +44 (0)1438 816267
Email: art@artvango.co.uk
Website: www.artvango.co.uk
Art Van Go also sells textile supplies

Angie Hughes
Ledbury Artplace
5a Worcester Road.
Ledbury
Herefordshire HR8 1PL
Tel: +44 (0)1531 633100
Email: angie@angiehughes.com
Website: www.angiehughes.com

Rainbow Silks
6 Wheelers Yard,
High Street,
Great Missenden,
Buckinghamshire HP16 0AL, UK
Tel: +44 (0) 1494 862929
Fax: +44 (0)1494 862651
Email: caroline@rainbowsilks.co.uk
Website: www.rainbowsilks.co.uk
Rainbow Silks also sells textiles supplies

The Beetroot Tree Gallery
South Street,
Draycott,
Derbyshire DE72 3PP
Tel: +44 (0)1332 873929
Email: info@thebeetroottree.com
Website: www.thebeetroottree.com

Ario
5, Pengry Road
Loughor
Swansea SA4 6PH
Tel: +44 (0) 1792 529092
Mobile: +44 (0)7877 709943
Email: ario@ario.co.uk
Website: www.ario.co.uk

Suppliers

In addition to Art Van Go, Rainbow Silks and Ario, which are listed above, the following suppliers are a wonderful source of materials for working with textiles.

nid-noi.com
Tel: +44 (0)1273 698112
Email: info@nid-noi.com
Website: www.nid-noi.com
Pelmet Vilene (Pellon), Heavy Pelmet Vilene Plus, CS500 and 800/Lutradur, Tyvek, Cello-Foil, Lamifix, play packs, threads.

Seawhite of Brighton Ltd
Avalon Court
Star Road Trading Estate
Partridge Green
West Sussex RH13 8RY
Tel: +44 (0)1403 711633
Email: info@seawhite.co.uk
Web: www.seawhite.co.uk

Index